THIS BOOK IS TO BE TAKEN *VERY SERIOUSLY* INDEED...

Do you ...

Worry that you're not silly enough?

*

Feel like you're missing out on the wave of silliness that's sweeping the country?

*

Feel under pressure to be "NORMAL"?

*

Enjoy fun more than work?

Then this is the book for you!

NOTE TO PARENTS:
THIS BOOK WILL KEEP THEM BUSY FOR HOURS!

Think of it as FREE BABYSITTING!

"The amount of eccentricity in a society has generally been proportional to the amount of genius, mental vigour and moral courage it contained. That so few people now dare to be eccentric marks the chief danger of the time."

—*John Stuart Mill, 1859*

I couldn't have put it better myself!

First published 2024 by Walker Books Ltd
87 Vauxhall Walk, London SE11 5HJ

2 4 6 8 10 9 7 5 3

Text, illustrations and photographs © 2024 Harry Hill

The right of Harry Hill to be identified as author of this work has been asserted in accordance with the Copyright, Designs and Patents Act 1988

This book has been typeset in Garamond 3 LT Std

Printed and bound by CPI Group (UK) Ltd, Croydon, CR0 4YY

All rights reserved. No part of this book may be reproduced, transmitted or stored in an information retrieval system in any form or by any means, graphic, electronic or mechanical, including photocopying, taping and recording, without prior written permission from the publisher.

British Library Cataloguing in Publication Data: a catalogue record for this book is available from the British Library

ISBN 978-1-5295-2098-9

www.walker.co.uk

MIX
Paper | Supporting responsible forestry
FSC® C171272

All activities are for information and/or entertainment purposes only.
Adult supervision is required for all activities.

How to be Silly Every Day of the Year

Or

365 SILLY THINGS EVERYONE SHOULD TRY ONCE

BY THE WORLD'S SILLIEST PERSON,
Harry Hill

Hi, I'm Harry Hill!

WALKER BOOKS

Hi!

This is my cat, Stouffer

A message from your Leader

8,344562 Short Street
Swaffham-Under-Arms
Kent

Dear Prospective Silly Person,

First of all, welcome to the world of silly! Thirdly, congratulations on purchasing this book – it may well be the silliest thing you do today! Ha ha! Gotcha! Your hard-earned money is now mine! But if I may be serious for a moment, I'd just like to say "Accountancy!"

I know what you're thinking: "Get on with it!" and "I want my money back!" and "I wonder if I can regift this book to my brother..."

Ahem...   (that's me clearing my throat).

⬛ ← And that's me clearing my pen!

The importance of being silly in life cannot be underestimated – just look at the government! Sorry! I promised myself I'd resist the urge to make cheap political jokes!

It's important to remember that life is short, so let's try and have as much fun between the serious bits – like homework and exams and visits to see your auntie in North Wales – oh, and the new drama your parents insist on watching every Sunday night after Antiques Roadshow.

PUBLIC HEALTH WARNING
SOME PEOPLE DO NOT LIKE SILLY PEOPLE!

Hard to believe, I know, but my advice is:

STEER CLEAR OF THESE PEOPLE!

I am Adrian Serious

I'm here to encourage you to become sillier because including a bit more silly in your life often involves thinking in a more creative way, not always taking the obvious route and thinking outside of the box. Although really your parents shouldn't be keeping you inside a box. I suggest if that is the case, you should call Childline — the number for them is 0798989142653876.

If you can think slightly differently to other people and see opportunities where others might not, you could very well be one of life's winners! I mean, look at me! I've got a pet hamster and a bike and a phone that you can also use as a camera.

Life isn't just about material goods, of course — although I've seen a really nice pair of shoes I like; the only problem is someone else's feet are in them. Anyway, enjoy the book, and do let me know how you get on via the address at the top of this letter.

Yours since-silly,

Harry Hill

President – The Royal Order of Upside-Down Snow Ferrets

Actually, that's the number of a fish and chip shop near me. I was just being ... er ... well ... silly ... but they do really good chips and lots of them, so do give them a call.

It gets busy around 7.00 p.m., so get in before that or there's a bit of a wait...

SERIOUS BIT

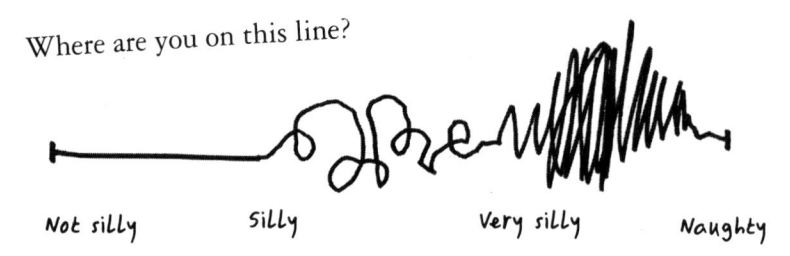

Where are you on this line?

Not silly   Silly   Very silly   Naughty

In some cases, it can be a fine line between being silly and being naughty. Most people will enjoy a bit of silliness, but everyone hates naughtiness, so if your idea of being silly involves permanent damage to property, injury, danger or unhappiness, STOP IMMEDIATELY! You have strayed into the bad world of naughtiness, and you're gonna be in BIG trouble. Even worse than that, you might get me into trouble, and we don't want that, do we? If I'm in prison, how am I going to come up with funny jokes and stuff for my shows? There are no TV cameras or theatres in jail (not sure why – after all, there's a captive audience)!

Knowing when to stop being silly

Tell-tale signs that you're being just TOO silly are:

1. Headache
2. Nose goes red and makes a squeaky sound when you touch it
3. Trousers fall down

Sometimes you've just got to take time out to be serious. I know, boring, right?

Times to be serious

1. Funerals **2.** Passport photos

(Those are the main two.)

Good, I like being serious.

Before you start!

1. You're going to need a lot of cardboard! So watch out for any cardboard boxes – particularly very big ones – and store them away for later.

2. Start collecting the cardboard tubes that magically appear at the end of a toilet roll. Believe me, you're going to need a lot of them this year. Collect them from all the toilets you go to, ask your relatives to save them, or maybe find out if there's someone in your street with a "dicky tummy" and go through their recycling? Kitchen roll works even better, because the cardboard tubes inside are even longer.

3. It's OK to skip the occasional day and come back to it. Actually, it's OK to just imagine yourself doing some of the silly stuff – after all, this has got to be fun, or what's the point? Oh, and make sure you have your pet adult on hand for any of the trickier activities.

OK, that's enough announcements – off we go!

DAY 1

Assess yourself

It's important to know just how silly you are at the start of this training programme so we can re-test you at the end and work out how well it has worked. If you're not very silly by the end of the book, then you may have to read the book again – and we don't want that. After all, there are literally more than twenty-five books in the world and if you read them all twice that will take you over a hundred years!

Answer these simple multiple-choice questions as best you can, then check your score at the back of the book to find out just how silly you are.

1. Where do you live?
   - ☐ In a house with carpets
   - ☐ In a house with no carpets or curtains
   - ☐ Up a lamppost

2. What colour is your hair?
   - ☐ Brown ☐ Bald
   - ☐ Green with purple spots

3. Where would you look to find the silliest person you know?
   - ☐ Swaffham town centre
   - ☐ 10 Downing Street
   - ☐ A mirror

4. What do you call someone who is hopping down the street on one leg, playing the trombone and kissing every dog they come across?

☐ Trouble   ☐ An interesting person
☐ Mum

1. ɯ, ɐsʃǝǝp!
ssʃɥ!

5. What position do you sleep in at night?

☐ On your side
☐ On your back with your thumb in your mouth
☐ Upside down

6. Who's your favourite celebrity?

☐ Fiona Bruce   ☐ Michael McIntyre
☐ Harry Hill

7. How often do you shout the word "knickers" in the supermarket?

☐ Never   ☐ Only if I'm looking for underwear
☐ Every time you go into the supermarket, especially if it's really busy

8. How silly do your friends think you are?

☐ What friends?   ☐ Quite silly
☐ Knickers!

9. When you walk down the street, do people

☐ Ignore you   ☐ Point at you and laugh
☐ Call the police

10. What goes up a chimney closed but not down a chimney open?

☐ Can you repeat the question, please?
☐ That's easy, an umbrella   ☐ Me on my day off

DAY 2

Give yourself a silly name

Before you start on the challenges contained in this book, you will need a new silly name. There are various ways to select a silly name, but I use the standard "make of family car, favourite animal, item of clothing" method. So, my silly name is Ford Parrot-Sock, and I'll thank you to refer to me as such from now on.

If you don't have a car, you can use the word "PISTACHIO". If your name is already Pistachio, then I'm sorry, I can't help you. This book is not for you.

You might like to come up with a different way to come up with a silly name, such as choosing random words from a book, or the first thing you see when you open your eyes. (I tried this, but didn't like the name "Mum Sitting-On-The-Toilet"!)

DAY 3

Make a silly scrapbook

It's really important that you document your year of silliness – it's also quite a silly thing to do (although it doesn't count as one of the 365 silly things – it's an extra).

So, when you're 105 years old like my mum (Hi, Mum! If you're reading this. Sorry I haven't been to visit for ... er ... five years ... but I've been writing a book about being silly – oh, you know that of course cos you're reading it. Also, Mum, I didn't get the cheque this month... Could you send another one please? Usual amount. Thanks, Your Favourite Son, Harry xxx), you can look back at your scrapbook of madness and nod your head wisely and say things like: "Hmmmm, I've no memory of that whatsoever" and "I wonder if I could get something for this old scrapbook on eBay..."

Once you've got your hands on a scrapbook, personalize the front however you like.

I've bought a scrapbook, Harry, but what will I put in it?

Good question!

You will be pasting in drawings, photos and some of the things that you will be making as part of your silly year. You might want to add doodles, drawings, cartoons and any silly ideas of your own. You can also use it to record the fun you had doing the various silly tasks and people's reactions to them. Keep an eye out for silly stories in newspapers and magazines and paste those in too. Find 'em, cut 'em out and paste 'em in your scrapbook!

DAY 4

Make my Silly-O-Meter

A good way to gauge how silly your achievements are is to make the Harry Hill patented Silly-O-Meter.

Take an A4 piece of card (or smaller, depending on what size your finger is) – the front of a cereal box works pretty well, especially if you then cover it in white paper. Draw two black lines at right angles to each other – like you get on a graph – and make a hole in the bottom* left-hand corner.

So far, so good…

Now we need to calibrate your Silly-O-Meter by telling a very silly joke to a friend.

Stick your finger through the hole and bend it so it's flush with the piece of card (see Fig. 1).

Then say something like: "What goes ninety-nine thump? An ice-cream man being mugged!" or "I went to the doctor and he said, 'Stand by the window and stick your tongue out.' I said, 'Why's that?' He said, 'I don't like the people next door!'"

As your friend laughs (and if they don't laugh at THOSE JOKES, then there's something wrong with their chuckle muscles and THEY need to see a doctor!), let your finger rotate up to the maximum level on the graph.

* Sorry for using the word "bottom". (Oops! Used it again!)

Right, you're ready to go! From now on, be sure to measure how silly each of the following activities are and make a note in your notebook.

Fig. 1

Silly-O-meter

Hole

Your finger

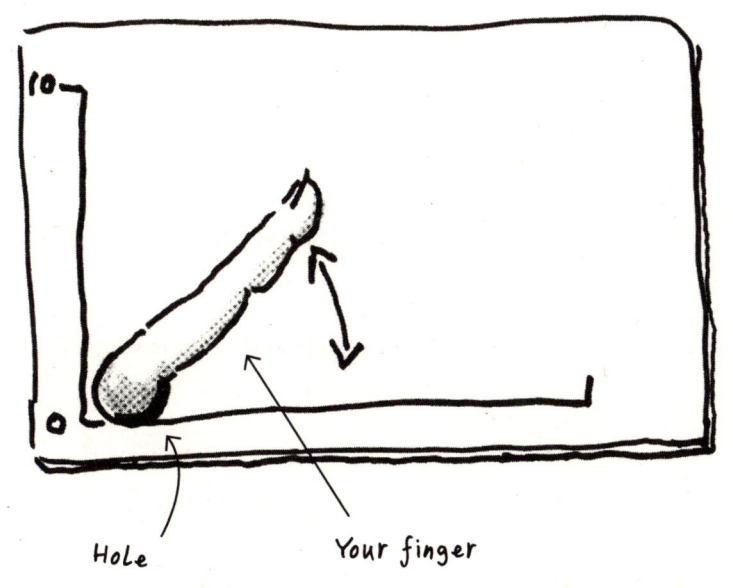

SILLY FACT NUMBER 1

Worms have no eyes, and yet this didn't stop a worm winning the Embassy World Darts Championship in 1997.
(Note to self: need to check this.)

DAY 5

Hold a hole digging competition

Stick up posters saying "HOLE DIGGING COMPETITION". Invite your friends and family to take part. Make it clear that points will be awarded for the depth and width of the hole and for a hole dug in a difficult-to-get-to place like under a deck chair.

If you have limited space – for instance, if you live in a flat with only a window box or pot plant – then you can stipulate that the hole be dug with a teaspoon or lolly stick.

Judging

If possible, get an elderly person to judge the holes as it seems that the older you are, the more interested you are in holes in the ground.

Prize

The digger of the winning hole gets to keep all the earth from all the other holes.

DAY 6

Create some Magic Mud

Take the earth you get out of the holes and put it in jam jars, then make labels claiming all kinds of special properties for your mud ... and try to sell it to a passer-by.

For instance...

* **Hair-Restoring Mud!** Rub it on your head to cure baldness. 
* **Anti-Stink Mud** Put liberal amounts of it under your arms in the morning to fix bad body odours.
* **Homework Protection Mud** Spread some on your homework and tell your teacher that you "dropped it in some mud". (Good luck with this one – see you in detention!)

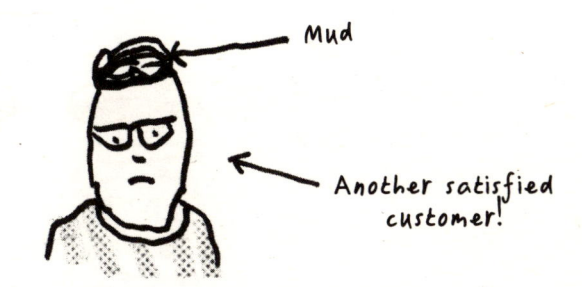

Day 7

Make an advert

Make an advert for the soil products you made on **Day 6**. Think about some of your favourite adverts and why you like them or why they're effective. Write a short script – think about the message you're trying to get across.

Write a list of all the props, wigs and costumes you need and where you're going to film it.

Draw a series of pictures, or storyboards, of what the film will look like, so that when you come to film it, you'll know exactly what you're doing.

If you can get your friend to help you with this, you could give them the credit of producer (you're the director).

Think about the music you're going to use on the advert.

If you don't have a camera, shoot it on a smartphone or tablet – there are plenty of simple apps to help you edit it and add music or a soundtrack. Keep it short! Most adverts are only about 30 seconds long – but a lot can happen in half a minute!

DAY 8

Think of a silly book

(Patio doors – get it?)

Make up some silly book titles – things like:

Bubbles in the Bathtub by IVOR WINDYBOTTOM	***Keeping Pairs of Animals in a Boat*** by NOAH ZARQUE	***Walking into the Garden*** by PATTY O'DOORS
Fun on the Beach by SANDY CHEEKS	***Old English Furniture*** by CHESTER DRAWS	***How to Beat Unemployment*** by ANITA JOB
Seeing into the Future by HORACE COPE	***Keeping Animals Clean*** by HUGH FLUNGDUNG	***Chicken Recipes*** by NORA DRUMSTICKS

Maybe design some book jackets for these silly books, or even, if you've got the nerve, go into a bookshop and ask whether they've got any of them in stock.

Excuse me, do you have "Fun on the Beach" by Sandy Cheeks?

NO! NO! NO!

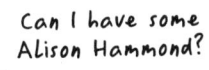

Create your own silly slang

DAY 9

Swap the names of stuff for the names of celebrities. For instance, water might become Miley Cyrus, chips might be Simon Cowell, ketchup might be Alison Hammond and sausages might become Justin Bieber.

So instead of "Mum, can I have sausage and chips with a dollop of ketchup and a glass of water?", you'd say, "Mum, can I have Justin, a portion of Simons, with a dollop of Alison and a glass of Miley?"

Before you know it, NO ONE WILL UNDERSTAND WHAT YOU ARE GOING ON ABOUT!

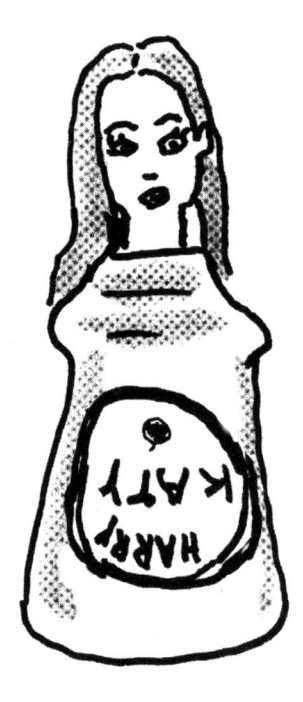

DAY 10

SILLY SCRIBBLES NUMBER 1

Draw a picture of a horse wearing flip-flops. What noise would it make when it walked along?

Can you direct me to the beach, please? (I'm wearing flip-flops.)

FLIP!
CLIP!
FLOP!
CLOP!

DAY 11

Have a fight with a chair

Ideally, put something soft on the floor – like carpet or a mattress – or have the fight outside on the grass. Start your furniture-fighting career by picking on a dining room chair then progress to an armchair or a sofa. Make sure you agree the rules first – no cheating! If anyone tries to tell you off, tell them, "The chair started it!"

1.
2.
3.
4.

DAY 12

Make a biscuit henge

Stonehenge is over 4,000 years old and took years to build – just think how much easier it would have been if they'd made it out of biscuits!

Get a packet of Bourbon cream biscuits and a photo of Stonehenge and off you go. When it's built, shine a torch through it and you'll get some idea of what it was like on that first summer solstice.*

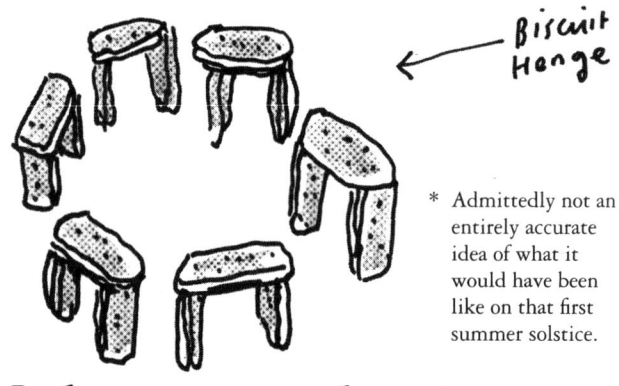

Biscuit Henge

* Admittedly not an entirely accurate idea of what it would have been like on that first summer solstice.

DAY 13

Make an everlasting snowman

Next time it snows, make a very small snowman (or snow ferret!**), and as the weather starts to warm up, pop him in the freezer before he has a chance to melt. Give him a bag of frozen peas as a pillow and bring him out next time it snows – that way he gets to last for ever!

AN UPSIDE-DOWN SNOW FERRET

** After all, I am the president of The Royal Order of Upside-Down Snow Ferrets.

DAY 14

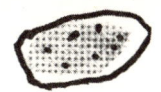

Make your own fortune biscuits

Hold those biscuits! What do you mean, "What biscuits?" The biscuits you used to build Biscuit Henge, of course! You've heard of fortune cookies? You know, the crackers that have a tiny piece of paper folded into them with some prediction or other written on them.

Well, we're going to make fortune biscuits. Cut up a few strips of paper that will fit inside a Bourbon cream biscuit. Write on them some silly predictions like:

> "You will go on holiday in the summer!"

or

> "When you ride your bike, the wheels will go round!"

Or, if you know who's going to be opening the fortune biscuits, you might be able to have some fun with it: "Hi, Dad! Can I have my pocket money, please?" or "Buy your child a bike for Christmas, or bad luck will befall you!"

Once you've written out your "fortunes", ask an adult to help you gently prise open the biscuits with a blunt knife. Place the slip of paper inside and squeeze them back together, then pop them on a plate and offer them round!

DAY 15

Hold a snail race

This is a silly thing you can do on your own or with friends.

Collect five or six snails.* Good places to look are upturned flower pots, rocks and any damp areas.

If all the snails look the same, you can mark them with a tiny piece of Blu Tack, or with a marker pen, taking care not to damage their shells.

Make up names for the snails, such as Lord Slimeford, Betty Fastmollusc or Shelly Shellsworthy, and talk to them to motivate them to win. Say things like: "Come on, Betty! You can do this!" and "You're gonna wipe the floor with the other snails, Slimeford!" or just "Win this race and I'll give you a nice big piece of cabbage, Shelly!"

Draw a circle about 75 cm wide on a patch of grass or cool, damp paving. Put the snails in the middle of the circle and place a flower pot or bucket over the top of them.

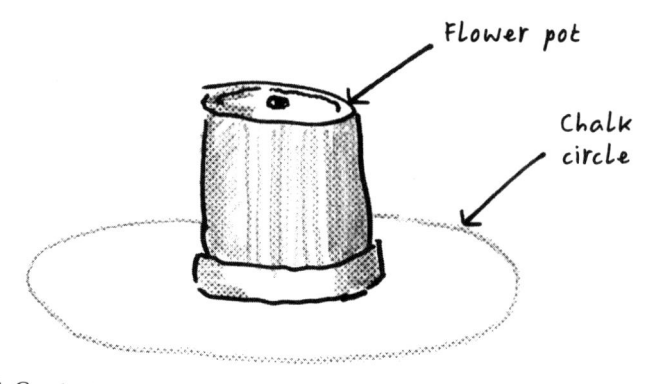

* Gently does it when picking up snails – they may be excellent racers but their shells are delicate! And make sure to wash your hands afterwards!

When you're ready for the race to start, blow a whistle, or make another loud noise,* lift the flower pot and watch them go! The first snail to reach the edge of the circle is the winner. Don't forget to encourage your snails to really go for it by shouting things like: "Come on!", "Get a move on, we haven't got all day!" and "The winner gets a big kiss from Gemma Collins!"

Note

Snails are quite slow movers, so this may take a little while.

Notey-note

Avoid holding the race in an area populated by birds such as the thrush, as this may result in the loss of some of your racers (thrushes eat snails). Similarly, do not hold a snail race in France (google "snails" and "French people" – yeah, I know, right? Yuck!)

Notey-note-note

Make sure you return the snails to where you found them once the race is over – otherwise word will get out amongst the snail community, and next time they may refuse to take part.

* See my other book: *How to Make Loud Noises Like Those You Hear on TV.*

DAY 16

Hold a smile-a-thon

Time how long you can hold a smile for. Sounds easy, doesn't it? Anything longer than four hours is good.

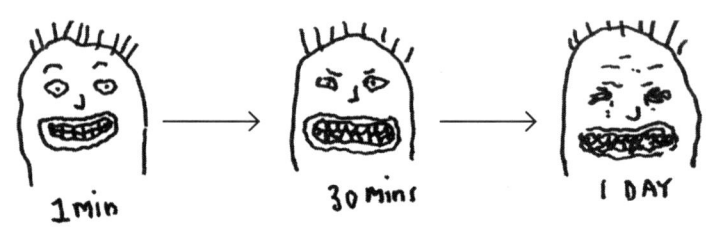

1 min → 30 mins → 1 DAY

But the last time my face ached so much from smiling was when I saw a giraffe trying to take off a roll-neck jumper!

DAY 17

Create a silly medical condition

Attach crisps to your toenails with Blu Tack and ask your mum whether you should see a chiropodist.

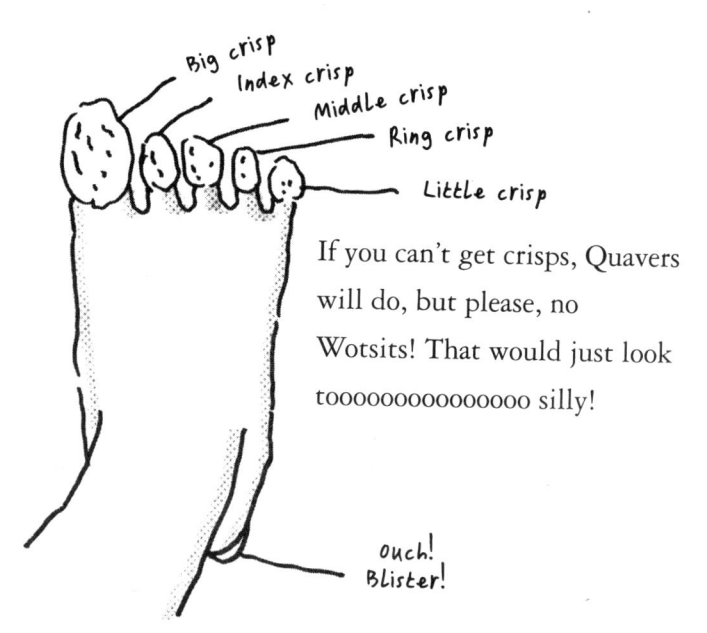

- Big crisp
- Index crisp
- Middle crisp
- Ring crisp
- Little crisp

If you can't get crisps, Quavers will do, but please, no Wotsits! That would just look toooooooooooooooo silly!

Ouch! Blister!

Make your very own Top Trumps

DAY 18

Write a list of your teachers and decide what scores to give them in the form of Top Trumps cards.

Score them for stuff like:

* Appearance
* Clothes
* Catchphrase
* Personality
* Hairstyle
* Sense of humour

But hey! Remember the first rule of being silly – don't be too mean, guys! Teachers have feelings too, you know!

Cut some white card into card-sized ... er ... cards and draw a picture of your teacher on each one with their scores underneath.

If you can't get white card, glue some white paper to some cardboard or to the backs of old Christmas or birthday cards. There's plenty of card about if you look! Now play Teacher Trumps with your homies!

DAY 19

Make a new friend

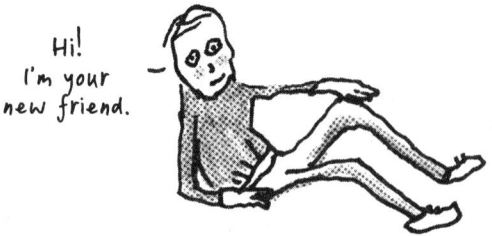

Hi! I'm your new friend.

When I say "make" a new friend, I mean MAKE a new friend – you're literally going to fashion another human being from other stuff!

You'll need:

* **Stuffing** – not sage and onion stuffing like you have with roast chicken. If you're thinking, "Yes, but I love the taste of stuffing!" OK, yes, I like it too, but that would mean eating your friend and what are you – a CANNIBAL? You need help!* No, the cheapest, easiest stuffing is scrunched-up newspapers and/or bubble wrap.

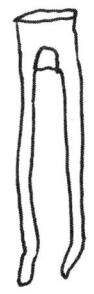

* **A pair of tights** (best) or trousers (not quite as good)

* **A paper bag** that is about the size of your head

* **A wig** – actually, you don't need the wig as some people don't have any hair (I know, weird, right?)

* **A long-sleeved top**

* **Parcel tape**

* **Pens or pencils**

* **Socks** – these are optional. Not everyone wears socks – e.g., Julio Iglesias (ask a grown-up), Olly Murs and Rita Ora.

* You may enjoy my other book, *Fifty Recipes for Cannibals*, which includes things like Kate and Sidney Pie, Ravioli – that's a lady called Ravneet cooked in olive oil – Beans on Toes and Roast IT Consultant with all the Trimmings.

Er ... can I have my stuffing back, please?

An angry oven-ready chicken

1. Stuff the tights, the top and the paper bag, and join them together – the easiest way is with parcel tape, but you could ask your friendly adult to help you tie or even sew them together.

2. Take your time drawing a face onto the paper bag; you might like to base it on someone well known – such as Benjamin Disraeli or Rihanna. You could even blow up an actual photograph of a celebrity face and stick it on. Pop the wig on, paint on hair or put a hat on your new friend.

3. Once they're complete, you can dress them in whatever clothes you like, or why not take them shopping for clothes at the charity shop or car boot sale?

My new friend

Me

Hey, that's my wig!

DAY 20

Make a photo-story of your new best friend

Photograph the new friend you made yesterday in everyday situations – waking up in bed in the morning, having breakfast, sitting on the loo! Then set up other situations – going to the shops, at the swings, riding a bike. Maybe take some selfies of you and your friend sitting eating crisps whilst watching TV (especially *Junior Bake Off*).

If you can, print off the photos and stick them in your scrapbook. Or you could maybe draw them. Here are some photos of me with my new best friend.

DAY 21

Find out how far you can throw a sausage

Next time you're having sausages for dinner, ask your mum or dad if you can borrow one. Then, go down the park and see how far you can throw it. Have a competition with your friends – but please no hot dogs, frankfurters or bratwurst as they have an unfair advantage due to their solidity. Make sure you wash your hands after this challenge – and put your sausage in the fridge – you're going to need it tomorrow.

DAY 22

Take your sausage on a skateboard

Retrieve yesterday's sausage from the fridge – it'll be like an old friend by now – place it on a skateboard, tie a piece of string to the skateboard and take the sausage for a walk. If anyone asks why you've got a sausage on a skateboard, say, "It was tired!" or "How else would it get around – it hasn't got any legs?" or "It's a shy sausage, so it's good for it to get out and about!" or "My sausage has a vitamin D deficiency, so it's crucial it gets some sun!"

If you can't get hold of a skateboard, use a roller skate, or a baby buggy or pram – or if you can't get anything with wheels, put it on a cardboard surfboard* and drag it around on that!

* See Day 147: Make a cardboard surfboard.

DAY 23

Make a house for a mouse

Make a fake mousehole and really freak out your mum. Everyone knows that a mouse's favourite place to live is in a hole in the skirting board – and who can blame them? We also know that your mum is scared of mice (well, my mum is!).

So, how do you make a hole without actually making a hole? Simple, we draw one. Choose a nice stretch of skirting board then take a piece of paper and draw a hole. Cut out the hole and attach it to the skirting board with some Blu Tack. To make it even more realistic, place a piece of brown wool on the floor as if it's the mouse's tail sticking out of the hole.

← Wool

Then sit back and wait for your mum... If you've got a way of videoing her reaction, even better!

Hi, I'm a sausage.

Have you seen my skateboard?

It's just that I'm not sure how I'm going to get home...

DAY 24

Start up a mouse cafe

You know the tiny white plastic tables you get free with every takeaway pizza? They make great tables for a mouse cafe! Put a couple of the white plastic pizza tables outside your fake mousehole and stick a sign above it announcing a new restaurant.

What's a good name for a mouse cafe?

* **Mickey's Place**
* **The Squeak Easy**
* **Scampers Hampers**
* **Chez Mouse**
* **C'est Cheese**
* **The Mouse Trap**
  (might put some mice off!)

I'm sure you can come up with a better one!

DAY 25

Camouflage yourself

Next time your parents have friends or relatives round, grab a few branches from a bush and tie them around your waist so that the foliage partially hides you. Then go up to people and say "Hello!" and ask them, "Sorry, can you see me OK?"

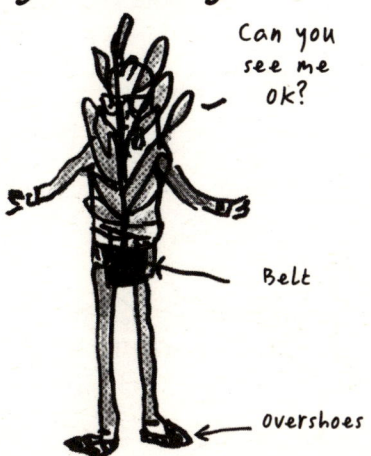

DAY 26

Make your own welding mask

What is welding, Harry?

Welding refers to "the uniting or fusing of pieces of metal using heat".

> ### You'll need:
> * Some cardboard
> * Scissors
> * Grey paint
> * Black paint
> * White paint
> * Tin foil
> * Some string to attach the mask to your head
> * An oxyacetylene torch (optional)

string — *Narrow slit to see out of* — *cardboard*

Hi, I'm a welder!

I know what you're thinking: "But, Harry! Welding is incredibly dangerous! There's no way my mum/dad/guardian/benefactor will let me do any welding!"

You are, of course, quite right. Which is why we won't be doing any welding.

Ha ha! Fooled you! Try asking your friends and family if they need any welding done. Then show them some examples of some of the designs you've made for welded wrought-iron work. Make sure you write down their reactions in your scrapbook!

Need any welding?

DAY 27

SILLY SCRIBBLES NUMBER 2

Draw a picture of a rabbit swimming away from a wasp. What's the rabbit saying? What's the wasp thinking?

Learn the ancient art of origami

DAY 28

Origami is the ancient Japanese art of paper folding. Using origami techniques, you can make flapping swans, dragons, fish, flowers and dinosaurs – but that takes a lot of practice, so instead we're going to make origami footballs. Take a piece of paper and carefully scrunch it up into a ball. That's it! Take the rest of the day off!

Origami football

DAY 29

Invasion ☺f the smiley p☺tat☺es

This is a great way to create excitement in your neighbourhood!

Simply take some potatoes – I'm thinking maybe six, but the more, the merrier – then give them eyes! Yes, I know potatoes technically already have what are referred to as "eyes", but they don't really look like eyes and … well … anyway … this is more fun.

The best eyes to give a potato are the googly ones you can get from craft shops (or online), but if that's not an option, draw eyes onto white paper or card and cut them out – this way you get to give your potatoes real personality!

Make your potato smile by telling him something funny, like, "What do you call someone with some fudge on their head? Brian Fudgehead." Or just draw on a smile with a felt-tip pen.

You might like to give your potatoes names like Alan, Beyoncé or Spud. You can also make whole families of potatoes. You then take your potatoes and leave them in odd places around your town!

Silly places to leave a smiley potato:

* By a pedestrian crossing button
* In with the carrots in the supermarket or greengrocer's
* Under "P" in a bookshop or library
* On a wall
* Looking out of the window of a train
* In your mum and/or dad's bed
* In your dad's shoes
* On a bench looking wistfully out over the setting sun. Maybe this smiley potato has another smiley potato friend with them…

Watch from a distance and you'll see that when people notice the smiley potatoes, they smile back!

Person BEFORE seeing a smiley potato

Same person AFTER seeing a smiley potato

Have a competition with your friends to see who can take a photograph of their potato in the most exotic or outlandish place. Paste the photos into your silly scrapbook. If you can't get your hands on potatoes, then you can use pebbles or rocks, but please, no aubergines.

DAY 30

Hold a funeral for a fly

Next time you see a dead fly,* give it a name, put it in a suitable coffin – like a walnut shell or a matchbox – and invite friends and family round for the burial. Some mourners might choose to bring flowers, but the dead fly might prefer a donation to a cause that was close to his or her heart, like the NSPCF.**

I'm not dead. I'm asleep!

Make up an order of service and write it out on some pieces of paper or card, ideally alongside a drawing of the fly. Things to include in the Fly Ceremony:

* **Songs**: sing a few fly-related songs like "Wind Beneath My Wings" or "Gonna Fly Now" (the theme from *Rocky*) or "I'm Like a Bird" by Nelly Birdtable.

* **A eulogy**: make up a story about the fly's life: "He was born a maggot in January 2023 and always loved buzzing around the park, looking for dog muck", etc.

DAY 31

Have a crying competition

Have a competition to see who's best at crying. Think of sad things like dead flies and bad shoes. Make sure everyone's got a hanky.

---

* Don't kill one! We're short of flies as it is!

** National Society for the Prevention of Cruelty to Flies (of which I am patron).

DAY 32

Make a gravestone for a fly

Your fly's grave will need a headstone, but it doesn't have to be a stone. It could be a pebble; it could be a piece of wood.

Write on the gravestone some details about the fly, things like: "He liked flying about" or "She got a real buzz from bad smells". Or make outlandish claims about the fly's achievements – things like: "Here lies Lily the Ladybird, who rescued her entire family from a burning building" or "Fred the Fly, Winner of *Flies Got Talent* 2024". You know … stuff like that!

DAY 33

Help to prevent further unnecessary fly deaths!

It's so sad to see flies trapped in spiders' webs just waiting to get eaten, isn't it? I mean, I understand that spiders have got to eat, but webs are so difficult to see; it doesn't seem very fair on the flies.

Let's make it more of a level playing field by putting up small warning signs near spiders' webs so the flies have got a fighting chance of avoiding certain death. Your warning signs might say:

WARNING! SPIDER'S WEB AHEAD!

THIS IS A SPIDERS' WEB WATCH AREA

SEE THE WEB, SAY THE WEB, SORT THE WEB!

DAY 34

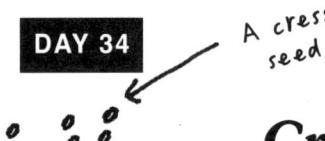

A cress seed

Create some messages in cress

This is a good way to communicate with people in tall buildings or planes, or with Richard Osmond.

Clear a patch of earth as big as you can get. This could be in your garden or, if you don't have a garden, it could be a tray of earth or a window box.

You'll need:

* A tray
* Some earth – easiest is potting compost, or, if you're really, really, really, really, really, really, really, really, really desperate, it could be earth dug out of the garden
* Cress seeds
* Grass seeds

What to do:

Decide on the message – OR "CRESSAGE" – you want to write in cress. It could be something like "Hello!" or "Go Away!" or "Caution! Uneven Surface!" It could just be your name, or a friend's name, or the name of your favourite football team (keep it clean, guys – there's no room for smut in the cress!). Or you could just sow a smiley face emoji. ☺

1. Sprinkle the cress seeds liberally in the shape of these letters.

2. Sow the grass seed in the gaps around the letters so that the whole patch (or tray) of earth is covered in seeds. Make sure you water it regularly or it'll dry out, the seeds won't germinate and you'll never get your cressage across.

3. After about two weeks, you'll have a lovely green patch of cress and grass. You might be able to read your message, but here's how you make it really clear: snip the tops off the cress with a pair of scissors, and suddenly, there it is: your message in white against the green of the grass. If you've grown the cress in your garden, it will be revealed when the grass is mown.

4. Take a photograph of it and stick it in your scrapbook.

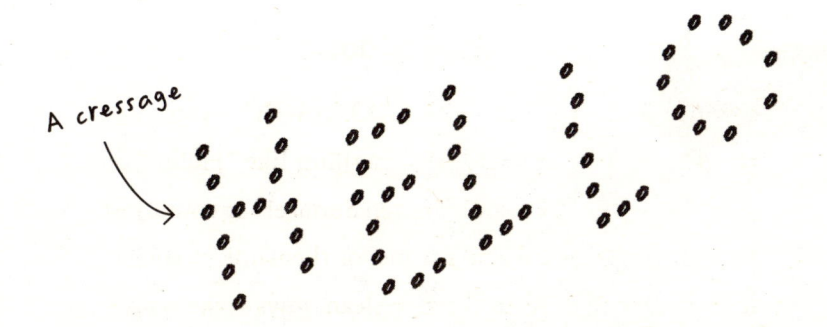

A cressage

DAY 35

Live off gravy

Live off gravy for a day! So that's just gravy. It can be chicken or beef gravy or even vegetarian gravy, so long as it's got the word "gravy" on the packet. No soup! No *jus*! Absolutely no *consommé*! This won't be very enjoyable, but you can be sure that tomorrow you'll REALLY appreciate your meals!

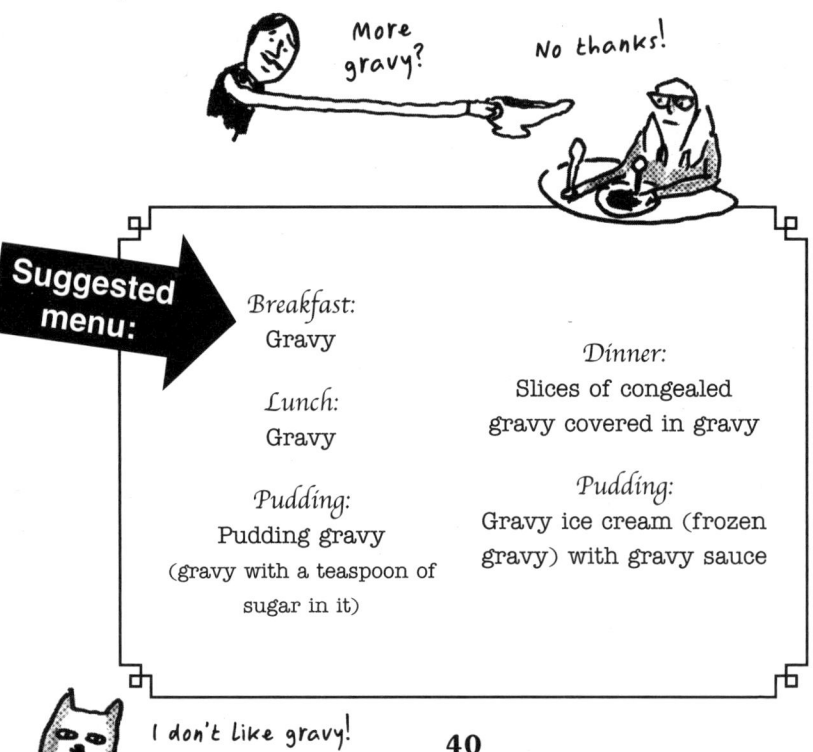

More gravy?

No thanks!

Suggested menu:

Breakfast:
Gravy

Lunch:
Gravy

Pudding:
Pudding gravy
(gravy with a teaspoon of sugar in it)

Dinner:
Slices of congealed gravy covered in gravy

Pudding:
Gravy ice cream (frozen gravy) with gravy sauce

I don't like gravy!

> **SILLY FACT NUMBER 2**
> A chair with only two legs is technically a very short ladder.

DAY 36

Extreme conditions board game

Try playing a board game in extreme conditions, e.g.:

* Monopoly in a thunderstorm
* Cluedo in a gale
* Chess in a flood
* Very hot conditions snakes and ladders

If you can't wait for the next extreme weather conditions, you can recreate them like this:

* **Gale** – get a friend to direct an electric fan at you.
* **Thunderstorm** – try playing Monopoly whilst having a shower.
* **Flood** – play chess in the bath.

DAY 37

You call that hopping?

Hop till you drop!

I'M HOPPING MAD!

Hop up and down in a crowded area like a supermarket, charity shop, car boot sale or wedding reception, going:

"Aaaah! Argh! Raaagh! Raaarrgh!"

If anyone asks you what's wrong – and believe me, they will – just say "I'm hopping mad!" Watch as they dissolve in a big old heap of laughter.

DAY 38

Start a silly campaign

Use your smiley potatoes from **Day 29** to start a campaign to stop people eating potatoes! Point out just how cruel chips are, not to mention jacket potatoes – these guys are baked alive, then slit open and eaten with butter! Stop the killing!

Write a letter to your local MP, send letters to your favourite celebrities asking them for their support and see how many reply! Stick the replies in your … yes, you guessed it … scrapbook!

> Here's a letter I sent to England football manager, Gareth Southgate:

a football (arrow to football doodle)

Dear Gareth,

How are you? I'll cut to the chase: have you ever thought about what it might be like to be a potato? Plucked from your home deep in the earth, skinned alive, then cut up and boiled or fried or even mashed?

I know what you're thinking, Gareth. You're thinking, "I wonder what's for dinner? I hope Mum is cooking chips again!" But that's exactly why I'm writing to you! We must stop this cruelty! Potatoes have as much right to a long and fulfilling life as Harry Kane or, er ... (sorry, I don't know any other footballers). That's why I'm starting a campaign: Save Our Spuds, or SOS for short. I need a hugely respected figure like yourself to spearhead my campaign.

You can start by having a word with Gary Lineker and asking him to stop telling people to eat crisps.

Your friend,

Harry Hill

PS *Good luck with the football!*

President – The Royal Order of Upside-Down Snow Ferrets

XXXXXXXXXX

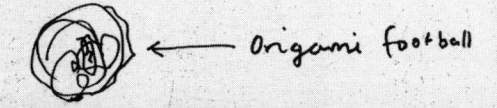

← *origami football*

> **DAY 39**

Surprise your family with a bit of Shakespeare

Shakespeare was a bald bloke who wrote a lot of plays about five hundred years ago. That's probably all you need to know about Shakespeare, but why not dazzle your friends and family by casually slipping a little bit into your conversation?

It's me, the bard!

Learn this quote from his play *Hamlet*, in secret, and the next time your mum or dad tells you it's time for bed, say:

> To sleep: perchance to dream.
>   Ay, there's the rub!
> For in that sleep of death
>   what dreams may come
> When we have shuffled
>   off this mortal coil,
> Must give us pause. There's the respect
>   That makes calamity of so long life.

Then say "Goodnight! See you in the morning!" and disappear off to bed.

DAY 40

Create QR mayhem!

You know how everywhere you look these days there are QR codes instead of printed things like menus or instructions? Annoying, isn't it? Especially if you haven't got a phone, or the battery's flat, or you just really, really, really, really would prefer to have a thing in your hands that you can read?

Well, try this: next time you see a QR code in a magazine, cut it out and keep it. Then when you're in a restaurant, put it over the QR code for the menu (you can print all kinds of QR codes off the internet if you have access). So instead of the menu, they might get the details of a website about welding.

SILLY FACT NUMBER 4
QR code stands for "Quite Reasonable" code.

DAY 41

Take a duck's lunch order

Bread please!

Take a clipboard and pen, go to the duck pond and take a duck's lunch order. It'll probably be "bread", but it might be "cheese and quackers".

Bread please!

cucumbers *orange* *pack of spaghetti*

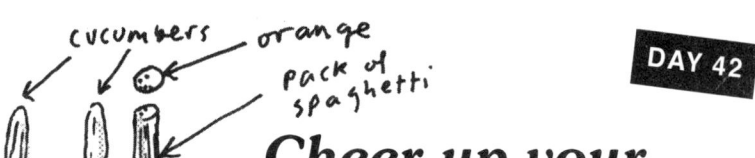

Bread roll

DAY 42

Cheer up your supermarket

It must get boring at times, working on the till at the supermarket. So let's try and keep those checkout operators entertained! Arrange your groceries on the conveyor belt so they spell out a message for the person on the till.

Suggested messages:

* Hi!
* Hello!
* Ouch!
* How much?!
* 1 + 1 = 2
* *In Xanadu did Kubla Khan*
  A stately pleasure-dome decree;
  Where Alph, the sacred river, ran
  Through caverns measureless to man
  Down to a sunless sea.

  (Good one for the big Christmas shop.)

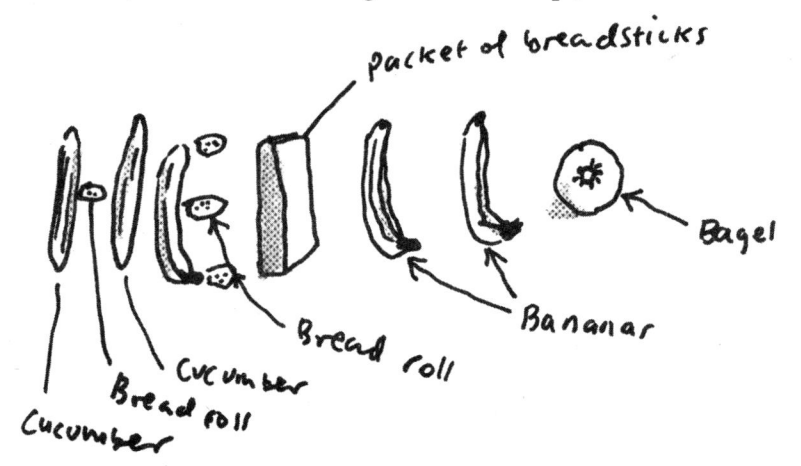

packet of breadsticks

Bagel

Bananas

Bread roll

Cucumber

Bread roll

Cucumber

Put a bit back

DAY 43

You know how normally you go to the supermarket and take stuff OFF the shelves? Well, how about taking an item into the supermarket from home and putting it ON the shelves?

The more bizarre the item, the better – a ceramic dog, a photo of your nan, a collection of old videotapes. Then ask someone who works at the supermarket how much the item is as "there's no price on it".

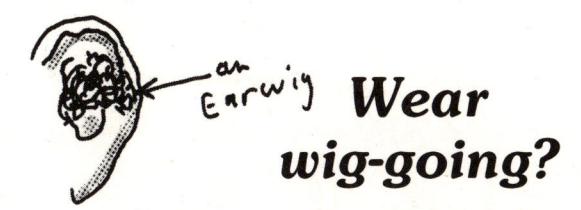

DAY 44

← an Earwig

Wear wig-going?

Put on a wig and go to the hairdresser's.

"I DO NOT WEAR A WIG!"

"Yes, you do, Adrian!"

DAY 45

Put new words to an old tune

There's loads of old songs and tunes that you could write your own words to – hymns, old music hall songs, classical music...

Actually, I wrote a song about the time I went to a drive-thru burger joint. I nicked the tune off a bloke called Frédéric Chopin – he wrote a song, but couldn't be bothered to come up with any words for it, which is presumably why he called it a rather silly name: "Nocturne in E Minor" – yeah, it hardly trips off the tongue, does it? No wonder it didn't make the charts.

I added my own words and gave it a snappier name.

Nuggets Nocturne

I bought chicken nuggets
For dinner
From the drive-thru,
But when I got home,
I realized I'd forgotten to pick up my complimentary drink.
I went back immediately to the drive-thru
And said, "Remember me? I came in earlier
And bought a meal deal."
But as I was trying to explain things,
I looked up and there it was still sitting in the hatch!

I leant out of the window
And I reached up to retrieve the drink cup,
But the person serving said to me,
"How do I know that drink's yours
and not someone else's?"
I said, "You can check the CCTV footage
And you'll see that it was me who ordered nuggets,
medium fries with a free cola."
He said he was prepared to
give me the benefit of the doubt,
But by the time I got the drink home it was warm.
So I just poured it away down the sink.
What a waste of time.

DAY 46

Could you hold this, please?

All you need for this is a ball of string or wool and the corner of a building.

Stand on the corner of your house and when you see your friend/nan/sister/teacher approaching, ask them whether they'll hold the end of your piece of string as you're "measuring the length of the corner for maths homework".

Adults always respond well to the mention of the word "homework". The other words they really like are "cup of tea", "lie-down" and "money".

Once you've persuaded your friend (although, by now, all your friends will have worked out that you're a bit of a wind-up merchant) to hold the end of the piece of string, go round the corner and ask someone else to hold the other end. Then quietly wander off, leaving the two each holding one end of a piece of string.

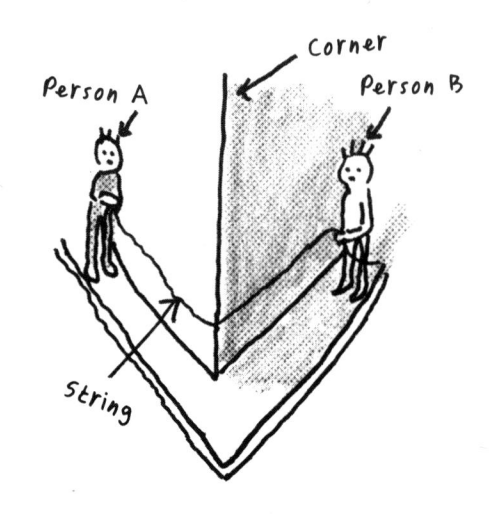

From a vantage point further away, watch what happens as it gradually dawns on them that they've been tricked!

DAY 47

Whistle while you work

Tape a whistle inside a vacuum cleaner hose.

You have to make sure the whistle is pointing the right way – in other words, backwards, because most vacuum cleaners suck, not blow! Then, when your butler next turns the vacuum cleaner on, ha ha! Talk about whistling while you work!

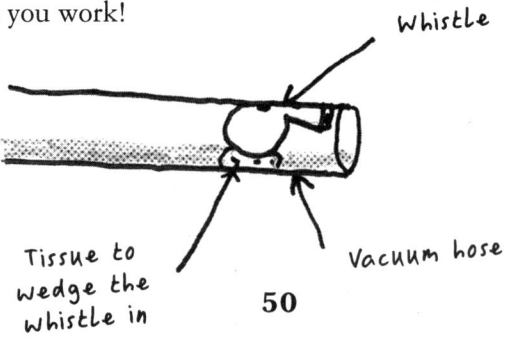

DAY 48

Become a surprise delivery!

You'll need a friend to help you on this one. Get inside a large cardboard box just outside your front door. Put a big label on the box with your mum or dad's name or whoever happens to be in the house at the time – it could be a friend's house.

Get your friend to ring the doorbell and hide.

Eventually, the person in the house will open the door. At this point, you burst out of the box and say something like: "Special delivery!" or "Surprise!" Or sing the words to "Postman Pat" or, even better, "Living in a Box" by Living in a Box.* Ideally, it would be really cool to film this so you can show it to your friends.

* OK, hands up, this is a very old reference. The group Living in a Box haven't had a hit since 1987. I'm not sure what happened to them but let's hope they haven't run out of money and now live in a … er … box.

DAY 49

Take a car door to "the drive-thru"

Make a car door out of cardboard. Go to your kitchen, lean out of the window and make your order!

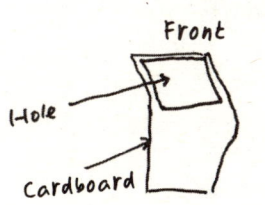

DAY 50

Stick in a tree

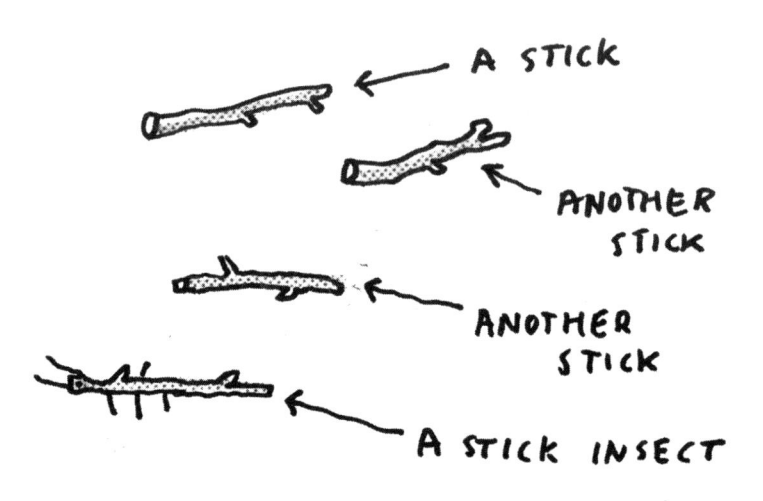

- A STICK
- ANOTHER STICK
- ANOTHER STICK
- A STICK INSECT

Look around the foot of a tree for any sticks that have fallen off it. Then see if you can return the sticks back to their rightful home, i.e., back in the tree. Throw the sticks up into the tree until they stay there. The tree will thank you for it and will be your friend for life.

SILLY FACT NUMBER 5

Snowmen don't cry. I know it sounds strange, as their lives are short and tragic. Despite this, you will never find a snowman crying, partly as they are extremely upbeat creatures but mainly because their eyes are made from stones and so do not have any tear ducts.

DAY 51

Become a tripod

Make a third leg by attaching a shoe to a broom handle and covering it with a trouser leg of similar design to the trousers you're wearing — the easiest to match are jeans.

Put on your longest coat, but only put your arm through one of the sleeves. Pad out the empty sleeve with screwed-up newspaper or bubble wrap, so it looks real, and tuck it into the coat pocket. You'll probably need a friend to help you with this.

Keep your spare arm inside the coat and hold on to the free end of the broom handle so you can operate the spare leg.

Once the coat is done up, it'll look like you've got three legs. See what reaction you get walking across the zebra crossing, wandering around the shopping centre, and, particularly, looking in the window of the shoe shop. If you've got the nerve (and I don't blame you if you haven't!), go into the shoe shop and ask, "Do you sell them in threes?"

DAY 52

EXTREME IRONING

Set up an ironing board in unlikely places and pretend to do your ironing.

Unlikely places to do your ironing:

1. The beach
2. The station
3. The front garden
4. The back garden
5. The park
6. Outside Buckingham Palace
7. Inside Buckingham Palace
8. The swimming pool
9. In a car
10. Gibraltar

DAY 53

Rub things up the wrong way

Get a sheet of paper – ideally a large piece of paper like A3* (or a length from an unused roll of wallpaper) – and some crayons, and go and find things to do rubbings of. Things like:

- Fire hydrants
- Entry phones
- Street signs
- Keys
- Tree bark
- Nan's face

*How come they give paper sizes the same names as roads?

DAY 54

Make a mould of someone's face

Tin foil →

Take a piece of tin foil and stretch it over someone's face – ask their permission first, or they might start to get a bit anxious! The result will be a foil mould of that person's face!

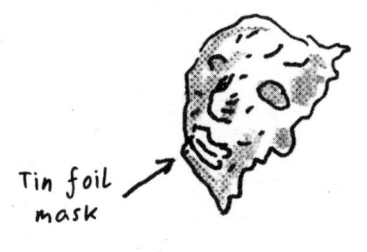

Start with your family and friends. If anyone asks why you're doing it, tell them you're going to use the mould to make a jelly.

← Tin foil mask

Who turned the lights out?

Label them up and stick them on your wall like a trophy hunter! Or flatten them and stick 'em in your scrapbook.

DAY 55

Make a silly magazine

Make your own silly magazine. Think of a good title for your magazine – the sillier, the better. Something like *The Sausage* or *The Snow Ferret* or just *Good Housekeeping*.

Gather together some magazines that your family have definitely finished with – you know the sort of thing: *Hello* magazine, *OK* magazine and *Not Too Bad* magazine.

> ### *You'll also need:*
> * Some A4 paper
> * Some paper glue – like PVA glue (none of that stinky stuff)
> * A pair of scissors

What to do:

You're now ready to enter the brilliant and fascinating world of collage! That's where you take printed images and combine them – and the fun will be in the way you do this.

So cut out a picture of somebody in one magazine then cut out the head of someone else from another magazine and glue it onto the body from the first. Arrange it on a piece of A4 paper and write about what's going on in the new collaged picture. It's easiest to just show you what I mean…

Silly sporting events

The Charles Dickens Foot Massager
"I love it! It soothes my feet!" says Charles D.

If you have access to a printer, copy the pages and circulate them around your friends — you'll be surprised just how funny other people find well-known people in silly situations!!!

If you don't have access to a printer, don't worry, it's a special one-off edition of your magazine and may be worth something one day!

Adrian serious

I DON'T LIKE IT!

I've imagined the underpants

(but know the feet.)

Make up a new sport

DAY 56

I don't know about you, but I've pretty much had enough of watching the same old sports on TV. So why not come up with a new one by combining two existing sports, such as …

- ***Tolf*** – a cross between tennis and golf. Played on a golf course but with a tennis ball and two rackets. The idea is to get the ball in the hole, but you only have one ball and take it in turns.

- ***Gennis*** – a cross between golf and tennis but with the emphasis more on the tennis. This game is played on a tennis court, but with golf clubs and a tennis ball. The aim is to … well, it's the same rules as tennis, which, to be honest, I've never fully understood. I mean, what's all that talk of love and juice, and why does it go up in fifteens and not ones?

- ***Snocker*** – a cross between soccer and snooker. Played with a full-sized football, but you're not allowed to kick it. You have to move the ball along by taking it in turns with a snooker cue, or if you can't get a proper snooker cue, then a broom handle will do.

You probably need to try some of these new sports out to find out which ones work best.

Anyone for TOLF?

DAY 57

Hold a tournament for your new sports

Round up a couple of friends and go to the park and play tolf, gennis, snocker, or whatever new sport you made up yesterday!

DAY 58

Bin heavy

Fill a black bin liner with bubble wrap or other lightweight items, then complain to your mum that it is too heavy to lift. Let her see you try to lift it – act like it's the heaviest thing you've ever tried to lift. Then watch as she uses all her muscles to lift it and almost falls over!

IT'S SO HEAVY!

OH! NO IT'S NOT!

Silly Fact No. 6

Horses won't sit down. Think about it. You see horses standing up, you see horses lying down, but never sitting down – even when they're watching TV.

SIT!   NO THANKS!

DAY 59

Redraw the globe

Draw a map of the world and imagine you're in charge of dividing it up and naming all the new countries.

Think of some silly names for existing countries and invent whole new ones!

I bet you can't come up with sillier names than the names of these ACTUAL places!

* Eek, Alaska, USA
* Fart, Virginia, USA
* Ugley, Essex, England
* Wagga Wagga, New South Wales, Australia
* Yum Yum, Tennessee, USA
* Brokenwind, Aberdeenshire, Scotland
* Crackpot, North Yorkshire, England
* Giggleswick, North Yorkshire, England
* Great Snoring, Norfolk, England
* Catbrain, Gloucestershire, England

DAY 60

Flag it up

Design new flags for some of the countries you've invented.

DAY 61

Draw a picture of the silliest person you know

If you ever doubt why you're on this journey, take a look at this picture to remind yourself.

Make someone smile

DAY 62

The next time you're being driven somewhere, hold up a sign that says "THIS CAR RUNS ON SMILES". See if anyone smiles back.

SILLY SCRIBBLES NUMBER 3

DAY 63

Draw a chicken sunbathing. What's she using as suntan lotion? What magazine is she reading? (Suggestion at the bottom of the page.)

SILLY FACT NUMBER 7

Dogs hate podcasts. Think about it. You sometimes see dogs watching TV or listening to the radio, but put a podcast on, and they always leave the room.

I really don't like podcasts!

Me neither! What's on TV?

← Silly scribbles suggestion:

cluck! Can somebody help me get the lid off the suntan lotion PLEASE?! *cluck!*

DAY 64

Give yourself a new smile

Do you look at your grandad and wish you could take your teeth out when no one's around just like he does? Yeah, me too! Well, now you can – this is an old trick but a good one.

1. Break an orange into quarters, then take off the four pieces of peel – this is what you're going to use to make your teeth.

2. Eat the orange – except the pips. If you eat the pips, you might end up with an orange tree growing in your stomach (this happened to my nan and it was very uncomfortable for her, but we didn't want to have it chopped down because we really liked the oranges that grew on it).

3. Take one segment of orange peel and cut it with a sharp knife* like so.

4. Then turn it inside out and stuff it in your gob. Hey presto! Suddenly you've got new teeth – just like Grandad.

* Sharp knives are sharp (the clue is in the name), so ask an adult to help!

5. In front of the mirror, practise saying things like: "I'd like to speak to a dentist, please!" and "Hello, my name's Rylan Clark!"

Smuggle in some silly words

COLESLAW 65

Choose a silly or unusual word or phrase and have a competition with your friends to try and include it in every lesson during one day at school.

Here are some of my favourite silly words:

- Coleslaw
- Pilchard
- Corn plaster
- Cuckoo spit
- Hum
- Knapsack
- Stickleback
- Stave
- Princely sum
- Cold cuts

So, you might be in a biology lesson…

YOU: "Excuse me, sir, but is there a stave on the stickleback?"

TEACHER: "What's that?"

YOU: "I was just wondering whether Knapsack had a princely sum on the cold cuts?"

Yeah?

PILCHARD!

COLD CUTS!

DAY 66

Make some silly badges

I'm lucky, I've got a badge-making machine, so I can churn out badges all day long!

Even without a badge-making machine, you can produce badges with a fairly good finish.

You'll need:

* Some white card, ideally. If you can't get fancy white card, use the brown cardboard of a cardboard box and glue white paper onto one side
* Sticky tape
* Pens/paints and some safety pins

What to do:

1. Decide what size badge you want to make, then draw a circle on the card by drawing round the bottom of a beaker, a coin, your sister's head or other suitable round object.

2. Then write on the disc whatever message you've got, or draw a picture or glue on a photo of your choosing. Tape a safety pin to the back of it, and off you go!

Some silly badges I have made:

- I'm too silly for this badge
- If you can read this, you're standing too close
- Nosy, aren't you?
- Bread please!
- I'm a member of The Royal Order of Upside-Down Snow Ferrets
- My other badge is even sillier!
- If you think I look silly, you should see my mum!
- Look out! I bite!

DAY 67

Make some chewing-gum ghosts

After you've chewed your chewing gum and extracted all the flavour, what do you do with it? Well, yes, you could stick it under your desk, but if you get caught, you'll be in trouble... You could fold it up in a piece of paper and dispose of it sensibly in a waste bin. Or you could shape it to look like a mini ghost.

Get a piece of card and write "Ghost Family Tree" on it in big letters. Every time you've finished chewing a piece of gum, stick it on the card, draw on two eyes and a mouth with a black marker pen and give it a name.

Pretty soon you'll have a whole family of chewing-gum ghosts.

Happy chewing!

DAY 68

Connect up some famous faces

You know at Xmas when your mum buys a whole load of Christmas cards? There are always a few left, aren't there? Why not take these spare cards and send them to celebrities, politicians or dignitaries and sign them from OTHER celebs? Imagine the look on the face of King Charles if he got a Christmas card from Donald Trump, or the lovely warm feeling Kylie Minogue would get if she got a Christmas card from Nicki Minaj?

Go ahead! Spread the Christmas love!

Suggested pair-ups:

* Harry Styles and Carol Vorderman
* Danny Dyer and the Duchess of Devonshire
* Alison Hammond and Idris Elba
* Kim Kardashian and Queen Camilla
* The Archbishop of Canterbury and Vin Diesel
* His Holiness the Pope and Basil Brush

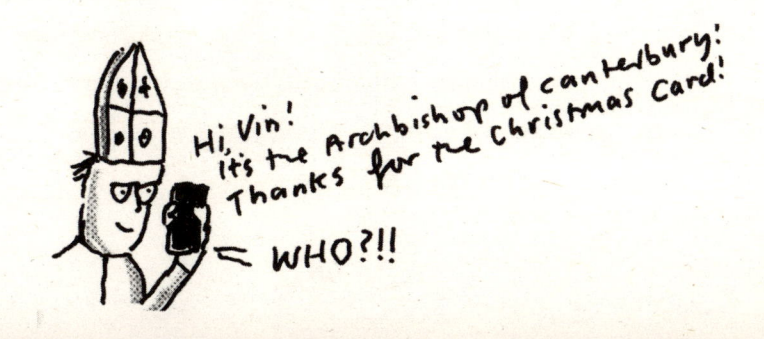

Day 69

Form a very silly club

A bit like synchronized swimming and robbing a bank, being silly is much more fun if you do it with other people. So why not form a silly club? Think of a suitable name for it, such as: "Shirley" or "The Silly Club" or "The ICOS" (International Club of Silliness), then:

* Write to the silliest people you admire most in the world and invite them to become members
* Design a membership card
* Come up with a secret handshake
* Design a logo and possibly even a uniform
* Have regular meetings and come up with a silly agenda for each one
* Appoint members of the club specific roles like: Sergeant at Arms, Treasurer, President, Vice President, Vice Vice President, Vice Vice Vice Vice Vice Vice Vice President and Keeper of the Ferret.

Day 70

Hold an AGM

Hold the very first Annual General Meeting of your Silly Society. Make sure you've got some soft drinks and some biscuits and ask all members attending to wear something silly. Here are the minutes from my own silly club meeting last weekend...

Minutes of The Royal Order of Upside-Down Snow Ferrets

<u>Attending</u>:

- President: Harry Hill
- Vice Vice President: Gary Hill
- Vice Vice Vice President: Harry's mum
- Treasurer: Ian the Information Worm
- First-Aid: Doctor Alan Bingham (Harry's old English sheepdog)
- Ferret Wrangler: Stouffer the Cat

- Harry's mum asked whether she had to carry three vices with her as they are made from solid iron and are very heavy, and she'd started to notice that her arms are slightly longer since she started carrying them. It was agreed that she could put them down.

- Ian the Information Worm asked whether Dr Alan Bingham, the old English sheepdog, was really a qualified doctor. An argument broke out when Ian demanded to see Alan's certificate, during which the goldfish bowl was knocked off the table. Cyril the goldfish got quite breathless for a bit, until Harry scooped him up and put him in his glass of water. Unfortunately, the water was fizzy and since then, Cyril has been farting a lot.

- Harry's mum cheered everyone up with her rendition of the Kelis hit "Milkshakes".

- Discussion about the weather for the annual Ferret-Wrangling Competition, which this year is to be held in Crackpot, North Yorkshire.

- Food fight.

DAY 71

Invent a silly walk

Why stick with the same old way of walking that you've been using all your life when you can develop a new and exciting silly walk? The masters of the silly walk are an ancient comedy act called Monty Python (look up "Monty Python's 'The Ministry of Silly Walks'" – it's very funny).

Here are some internationally recognized silly walks you can try.

* The Skip Dongler
* The Fortescue Pedogoggle
* The Cyril
* The Whippywobble
* Das Bizzle Schpitz (not for beginners)

A silly walk

DAY 72

Give the ducks meals on wheels

Put a slice of bread on a remote-controlled car and drive it past the duck pond. See how the ducks react. If you can't get a remote-controlled car, just use a toy car or a skateboard and pull it along with a piece of string. If you can't get one of those, then put the bread on a cardboard surfboard.*

Bread please!

* See Day 147: Make a cardboard surfboard.

DAY 73

Bounce a flip-flop

You'll need to go outside for this. Get two lengths of thick string – about five metres long – and thread them through a flip-flop. Get a friend to hold one end of each of the two lengths of rope and you hold the other ends.

Put the flip-flop up one end and pull the rope tight. Then, still holding the ends of the rope, suddenly outstretch your arms – this will send the flip-flop towards your friend. He then opens his arms and sends it back to you. Hours of silly flip-flop-based fun! It doesn't have to be a flip-flop either; it could be anything you can thread on the rope, like a plastic mug or a stale bagel.

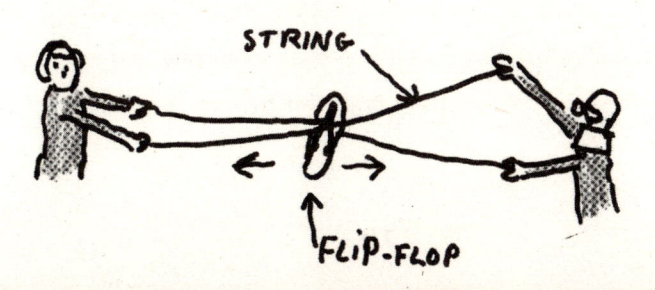

STRING
FLIP-FLOP

DAY 74

Chicken legend

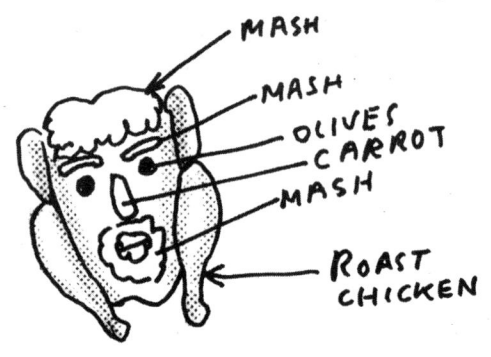

Next time you're having roast chicken, ask whoever's in charge if you can decorate it to look like the international singing star and one-time judge of ITV's *The Voice* – Sir Tom Jones. There's something about Tom's face that lends itself to being immortalized in this way.

You'll need:

* A roast chicken
* Mashed potato
* A piping bag
* 2 black olives
* A strip of red pepper (about 5 cm long and 1 cm wide)

What to do:

When the chicken's cooked and cooled, simply pipe the mashed potato to look like Tom's hair, eyebrows and beard, then use two blobs of mash for his eyes and pop the black olives on top of them. Ask an adult to help you carve a rough lip shape out of the red pepper and add that as Tom's mouth. You'll find that through half-closed eyes it looks just like Sir Tom is in the room. Here's a chicken-related Tom Jones playlist:

- "It's Not Unusual (to Eat Chicken)"
- "Help Yourself (to My Chicken)"
- "Funny Familiar Forgotten Chicken"
- "Mama Told Me (Not to Drumstick)"

NOTE:
With just a little tweaking, this could also look like Paul Hollywood.

SILLY FACT NUMBER 7

Post boxes are officially the property of the King, and sticking googly eyes on one is therefore punishable by life imprisonment in the Tower of London, which would be pretty cool. In fact, I'm writing this from the Tower of London, so next time you're passing, don't forget to wave.

DAY 75

Launch a leaf lottery

Number all the leaves on a tree (you will need the help of a very tall person). Obviously, this is much easier with a very small tree, or a bush.

Make bingo cards with the numbers of the leaves on and hand them out to your family. When autumn arrives, cross off the numbers as the leaves fall off. Or pick one each and have a competition to see who picked the leaf that falls off the tree first.

You could award a small prize for the winner – like a sweet, or a week off doing the washing-up. Plus they get to keep the leaf.

DAY 76

Design a silly theme park

Invent your own silly theme park and draw a plan of it. The first thing to decide is: what's the theme?

If Lego can have its own theme park, why can't cheese, or teddy bears or *Eastenders*? It could be literally anything!!!

Think about what would be in the theme park – the rides, the cafes and restaurants, and don't forget the gift shop!

DAY 77

Play Lettuce! Litter! Lotto!

Lettuce

This is the perfect silly thing to do because not only is it very silly, but it also helps your local environment. On your way to school, or the shops, or anywhere you like, pick up an item of litter that takes your fancy.*

> **You'll also need:**
> * A lettuce leaf
> * A discarded lottery ticket or used scratch card
> * Someone to play the game with

Got those? Good. You're now ready to play Lettuce! Litter! Lotto! When you meet your friend, say, "Lettuce! Litter! Lotto!", at which point, you both reach into your pocket or carrier bag and produce one of the three items – calling out what it is as you do so – "Lettuce!" or "Lotto!" or "Litter!"

Litter

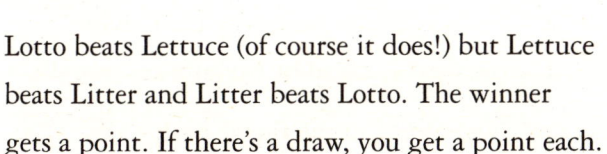

Lotto beats Lettuce (of course it does!) but Lettuce beats Litter and Litter beats Lotto. The winner gets a point. If there's a draw, you get a point each.

Lotto

Why not choose three things that have the same first letter and come up with your own version of the game?

* Please don't pick up anything sharp or mouldy – probs best to stick to plastic bottles and crisp packets. Oh, and make sure you wash your hands after touching litter. Yuck!

DAY 78

Write a silly story

Here are some suggested titles:

- Monsieur Fabrique – The Stain Detective
- The Invasion of the Cucumbers
- The Night I Coughed Up a Whole Caravan Site
- One of My Feet Is Talking to Me
- My Sister Ate an Elephant
- My Life as a Bacterium in Harry Styles' Stomach
- Snazzy the Caterpillar
- Shrimpy Thing and the Photocopier

I know what you're thinking: "That sounds like a lot of work, Hazza! I thought this was supposed to be fun, not homework!"

Yes, OK, fair enough. If you don't feel you've got the time to write an original silly story, why not take an existing story and change some of the words? So, *Little Red Riding Hood* would become (I've crossed out the words I've swapped for new words)…

WIDENING FOOT*

LITTLE RED ~~RIDING HOOD~~

One day, Little Red ~~Riding Hood~~ [Widening Foot] went to visit her ~~Grandma~~ [dentist]. She set off through the dark ~~forest~~ [tunnel] carrying a basket of ~~cookies~~ [fidget spinners]. On her way, she met a ~~wolf~~ [Bettaware salesman], who asked her where she was going. "I'm going to visit my ~~Grandma~~ [dentist]," said Little Red ~~Riding Hood~~ [Widening Foot].

The ~~wolf~~ [Bettaware salesman] ran to the ~~Grandma's~~ [dentist's] house, locked her up in the ~~wardrobe~~ [toilet] and got into the ~~Grandma's bed~~ [dentist's bath]. A little later Little Red ~~Riding Hood~~ [Widening Foot] got to the ~~Grandma's~~ [dentist's] house and looked at the ~~wolf~~ [Bettaware salesman] in her ~~bed~~ [bath].

"What big ~~eyes~~ [eyebrows] you have, ~~Grandma~~ [Dentist]!" said Little Red ~~Riding Hood~~ [Widening Foot].

"All the better to ~~see you~~ [play table tennis] with, my dear!" said the ~~wolf~~ [Bettaware salesman].

"My, what big ~~ears~~ [lips] you have!" said Little Red ~~Riding Hood~~ [Widening Foot]. "That's because I've had lip fillers from a very cheap cosmetic surgeon!" ~~"All the better to hear you with!"~~ said the ~~wolf~~.

"And what big teeth you have!" said Little Red ~~Riding Hood~~ [Widening Foot].

"All the better to ~~eat you~~ [advertise my dental practice] with!" said the ~~wolf~~ [Bettaware salesman] and tried to ~~eat her~~ [sell Little Red Widening Foot a pack of three dishcloths].

A passing ~~woodcutter~~ [hairdresser] heard a scream and ran to the ~~Grandma's~~ [dentist's] house. He hit the ~~wolf~~ [Bettaware salesman] over the head and released the ~~Grandma~~ [dentist] from the ~~wardrobe~~ [toilet].

The ~~wolf~~ [Bettaware salesman] ran off, and they never saw him again. Little Red ~~Riding Hood~~ [Widening Foot] went home and lived ~~happily~~ [like a very silly person] ever after.

The End

* Her foot is red and swollen, presumably due to some sort of insect bite.

DAY 79

Turn your unwanted teddy into a rug

It's not very nice to have real fur rugs any more, is it? Particularly the ones where they leave the head on – YUCK! No, but what if you really like the fur rug look ... and you're a Barbie – or possibly an Action Man – who's interested in interior design?

Why not turn your unwanted teddy bears into rugs?

Obviously if you're reading this and thinking, "Wait a minute! I love all my soft toys! I just can't get enough of them! Every morning, I wake up and long for more soft toys!", then maybe this challenge isn't for you, and I'm giving you permission to skip it.

Otherwise .... simply take your your teddy bear, ask an adult to help you make a slit in his belly (sorry, Mr Teddy Bear!) and remove the stuffing from his body. Flatten him out – maybe even iron him on a low temperature (get an adult to help with this) – and, hey presto – you've got yourself a top-of-the-range fake fur rug.

Day 80

Hold a toilet roll race

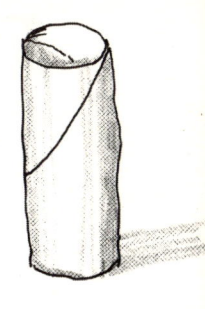

This requires at least two players (obvs).

* Select a toilet roll of your choice.
* Customize the outside of your toilet roll with slogans like: "Go faster!", "Watch me go!" and "Number one every time!"
* Stand at the top of the stairs, and, after a suitable command ("On your marks, get set, roll!" is a good one), release your toilet rolls.

The winner is the first toilet roll to the bottom (if you excuse the expression).

WARNING!

This might annoy your parents, so best to:

* Not tell them.
* Wind the toilet roll back up onto its cardboard roll afterwards (tricky).
* Buy your own toilet roll.
* Ask for a toilet roll for your birthday (but that's a bit weird).
* After the race, hide for a week.

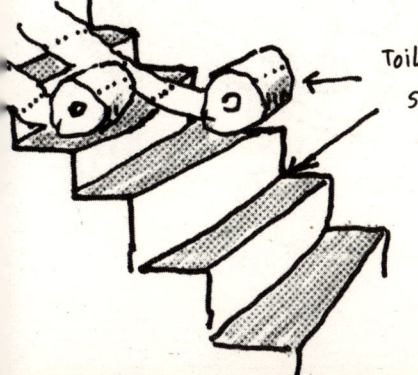

Toilet roll race

DAY 81

Who's got the longest toilet roll?

After the race yesterday, see who's got the longest toilet roll. There's no prize for this, but it's useful to know. If you're feeling really SENSIBLE, you could count the number of sheets in your roll and divide the cost of the toilet roll by that number to work out the cost per sheet. I suppose you could then work out how much it costs every time you go to the loo, but I wouldn't recommend it.

I like being sensible...

DAY 82

Make a selfie board

Everyone loves a selfie, right? So why not try turning selfies into hard cash with your very own selfie board? Take a piece of regular cardboard and cut two face-shaped holes.

Above the holes, write "SELFIES £1.00" – I mean, this is what I charge for a selfie, but then I'm an award-winning comedian and TV star, so you might have to lower your prices. Then wander around the playground and see if you can get anyone interested.

DAY 83

Make some silly wanted posters

Draw a picture of a mosquito and make up a wanted poster. Add the details of the "offence" ("Wanted for biting, causing minor skin irritation and buzzin'") and ask anyone with any information to report to the Spider Police. Put the posters up and see if anyone comes forward with info.

WANTED
CHERYL
THE MOUSE

I may have eaten Cheryl.

SILLY FACT NUMBER 491

When you hear that a whale has beached itself, usually it's because they have come into the shallow water because they heard an ice-cream van. Whales love ice cream. Their favourite ice creams are: 1. Fish Calippo, 2. Plankton Magnum, 3. Krill Twister, 4. Lemonade Sparkle with a sardine on top.

I fancy a choc-ice.

Get me a Calippo.

DAY 84

Make your own pea-shooter

DON'T SHOOT ME!

A PEA

You can obviously buy a professional-level pea-shooter from one of the many online shopping stores, but some of you won't yet have achieved professional pea-shooting status – i.e., earning a living from shooting stuff with peas. So, I recommend using those wide straws that you get when you buy a milkshake. Usually, if you ask nicely, you can get the shop owner to give you a couple. Or you can just grab a couple, but don't drag me into it if you get caught.

You might like to customize your pea-shooter with patterns or pictures of well-known pea shootists – like Lizzo, Bear Grylls and former Labour Health Secretary Alan Milburn. Write some motivational style slogans on the side of your shooter – things like "EAT PEAS, SUCKER!", "YOU LOOK LIKE YOU'RE DYING FOR A PEA!", "GIVE PEAS A CHANCE!" and "PEAS OR GLORY!"

Obviously, you can use peas as ammunition – I mean, it is a pea shooter after all – fresh peas, frozen peas, but please, no mushy peas, as that's just really messy.

Personally, I prefer to use my own homemade mushed-up paper pellets. There are a couple of ways you can make these — you can chew paper until it's mushy, or you can soak paper and mush it up with a fork. Once it's of the correct consistency — moist but not too mushy — you can make it into pellets. When wet, these are great because they're more likely to stick to your target, but that might also get you into trouble, so don't tell me I didn't warn you.

Make your own targets — they could be the usual circles-within-circles, or I like to use a photo of my archenemy, Mr Evans, who is the traffic warden in my street. If you can't print off a photo, cut one out of a magazine — you could have lots of different faces on one target and award points for each one, or you could award a different number of points depending on where in the face you hit them.

A cheap but not entirely satisfying alternative is a Rice Krispie fired out of a paper straw. I say not entirely satisfying as it really does no damage whatsoever. Also, the Rice Krispie won't stick on the target's face unless you cover the picture with hair gel first, which isn't always an option.

DAY 85

Take a silly survey

Get hold of a clipboard – or a piece of cardboard with a couple of paper clips will do. Hang around a brick wall and, as friends pass, ask them:

"Hello, I'm doing an important survey. If you had to choose … what's your favourite brick?"

Then point to the wall. Ask for their reasons. Maybe you can think of some other silly questions to ask? Maybe take your selfie board (see **Day 82**) with you and see if you can sell some of those too.

DAY 86

Help the world to see

Remember the googly eyes you bought on **Day 29** for your smiley potatoes? You've probably got a few left. If not, you can always draw some more, and this time, make some bigger ones because we're going to stick them on things that don't have eyes but deserve them, like post boxes, the ticket machine at the car park (this is a good one as when the ticket comes out, it looks like it's sticking its tongue out!) and front doors.

84

DAY 87

Draw a three-word picture

Open a book at a random page. It's better if it's a textbook (sorry, I know, boring!) or an encyclopedia. Close your eyes and put your finger on the page. Write down the word your finger is pointing to.

Do this three times. Draw a picture that includes these three words. (Or you could go on the What 3 Words app and enter a location that means something to you – your friend's house or the site of your favourite fast-food restaurant – and draw the three words that are linked to that location).

Here are some suggestions to start you off:

* Royal Hatch Bush
* Fuse Stuffing Forgets
* Mining Intro Marble
* Boot Chin Cactus

BOOT CHIN CACTUS

SILLY PEOPLE FROM HISTORY NUMBER 432: HENRY PAGET

Paget (1875–1905) made his car exhaust release perfume as he drove along! I wouldn't mind getting stuck in a traffic jam behind Henry!

HENRY CYRIL PAGET
5TH MARQUESS of ANGLESEY

DAY 88

Topiary for beginners

What's topiary? Well, it's not cutting your toenails into different shapes – as I first thought – that's toepiary. It's actually trimming bushes and hedges to look like animals and geometric shapes and, well, anything you want.

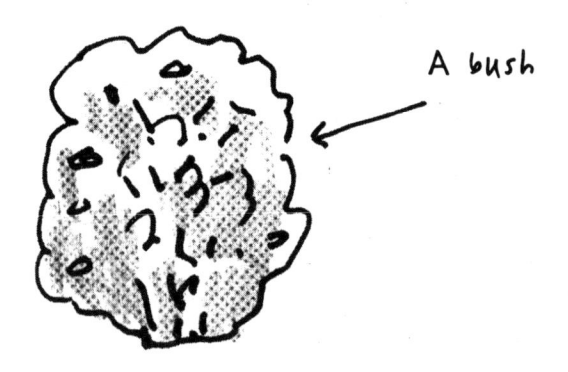

A bush

Now, obviously, hedges and bushes take ages to grow, so you can't really practise on them, so I'm suggesting you start on broccoli, which looks a bit like a bush and is something you should be able to get your hands on – what parent would say "no!" if their son or daughter asked, "Can I have some broccoli?"

How to do topiary

Maybe take a look at some real topiary first. Perhaps there's a stately home nearby with some bushes that have been cut to look like peacocks or something … or if it's raining, just google it.

Some shapes that I'd recommend for broccoli topiary:

- * Peacock – tricky but very rewarding
- * Nan's head – because the top of broccoli looks a bit like Nan's hair, right?
- * Teapot
- * Squirrel
- * Boris Johnson – I dunno, there's just something about his face that suggests a wild, untamed bush.

Once you've decided, use a pair of scissors to snip all the broccoli away that doesn't look like the shape you're going for. That's it! Easy peasy lemon squeezy, my mum's feet smell rather cheesy!

A BUSH THAT LOOKS LIKE A TEAPOT

A TEAPOT THAT LOOKS LIKE A BUSH

DAY 89

Become a town planner

You're probably like me and think that a lot of the roads round where you live have rather boring names that don't necessarily tell you anything about what they're like. Things like the high street – we all know that it's no higher than any of the other streets. Coronation Street – coronations take place in Westminster Abbey, not in Manchester. I mean, I could go on. What's the answer? Well, rename the streets!

Draw a map of your local area and give the roads the sort of names you think are suitable.

For instance...

If there's a particular road where everyone dumps old mattresses, call it Mattress Corner. If there's a road with a lamppost in it that all the dogs like to use, maybe that road should really be called Dog Wee Alley?

This doesn't just apply to streets and roads but to parks, rivers and bridges. Let's rename the whole town!

Here's a map of my area with the streets I've renamed:

DOG MUCK ALLEY
BAD SMELL MEWS
TWIX WRAPPER LAKE
SKIP STREET
MATTRESS MEWS
WEIRDO LANE
RD

MAP OF MY AREA

Make a silly Easter bonnet

DO YOU LIKE MY HAT?

NO! — sez A. SERIOUS.

It's nearly Easter! Everyone's going around singing songs about Easter bonnets, so why not make your own very silly one?

To make your hat, take a piece of cardboard, coil it round your head. Hold it together and lift it off your head. Ask a friend to help staple the ends together and you've got yourself a hat!

Now paint stuff onto the hat — any silly slogans or pictures you like. Glue a load of stuff onto the hat: photos from magazines, beer mats, dog biscuits — you know, something for everyone! Maybe make a theme for it, like: "My Favourite Things" or "Ducks".

I'm going as a Drawing Pin.

DAY 91

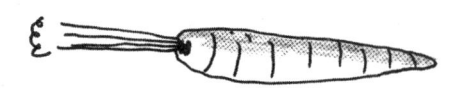

Welcome to Veggie Land

Next time your mum or dad heads off to the supermarket, or artisan greengrocer's, give them a long list of all the vegetables you'd like them to get. Things like carrots, parsnips, turnips, corn-on-the-cob, broccoli...

I know veg is expensive, but what parent ever said, "No! I'm not buying you any fresh vegetables!" They might be suspicious and say, "What do you want all this veg for?"

I'm afraid you'll have to work out your own answer to that. Here's what I told my mum: "I'm making a ratatouille." Then, when I didn't actually make the ratatouille, I told her: "Yeah, I couldn't get hold of a fat enough rat!" That seemed to do the job.

The truth is, you want it because you're going to make a city entirely from vegetables.

Get a large tray or a piece of board and just start building your cityscape.

Here are some tips for what works best:

Rock? or POTATO?

* **Multigrain crackers** make great roads and pavements.
* **Celery** with the leaves still attached makes great trees.

* Tops of **carrots** and **kale** make good shrubs and bushes.
* **Broccoli** makes great trees – pack a few of them together and you've got yourself a forest.

TREE or BROCOLI?

- A whole **pineapple** makes a good tropical palm tree.
- You can make hills from big loaves of rustic-style **bread** (it's not so effective with a sliced loaf!).
- **Large potatoes** make good rocks; **cabbage** and **lettuce** leaves laid flat make great fields.
- Give your veggie city a name. I called mine Las Veggies.

Draw a map of Veggie Land

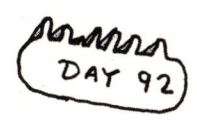

DAY 92

Draw a map of your veggie city and name all the roads and parks and hills. Why not extend the city in your map to include some other buildings like theatres, restaurants and racetracks? Here are some names for places:

- Celery Walk
- Lettuce Lane
- Broccoli Park
- Carrot Creek

DAY 93

Top secret face-off

Leave a book or file around with TOP SECRET! and PRIVATE PROPERTY! written on it. Inside the book, put a photo or drawing of you pulling a face and sticking your tongue out. Then when someone takes a sneaky peek, they'll know that you know what they're up to!

DAY 94

Make a root toot!

Take some of the carrots you chopped the top off in your veggie cityscape and see if you can make them into whistles. Yes, you heard me right: you're going to attempt to make a whistle from a carrot!

How to make a carrot whistle:

1. Get a medium-sized carrot. Ask your favourite adult to chop the other end of the carrot off and to drill a hole right down the middle of the carrot.*

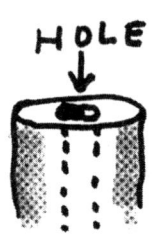

2. Ask them to use a sharp knife to cut a wedge out of the carrot (about 1 cm from the thicker end) and carve out a small hole to make an air hole.

Cut out a wedge

* Do not try this on your own as it's extremely dangerous and you might end up with holes in your hands!!!

3. Cut a 1 cm length out of the smaller chopped-off end of the carrot, then trim it so it fits snugly in the hole drilled in your bigger carrot.

4. Wedge this smaller carrot cork in the hole.

5. You're ready to go! Blow down the thick end of the carrot and you should hear a whistle! If your adult has still got their drill out, get them to drill some holes along one side of the carrot and you've now got a carrot that plays lots of different notes.

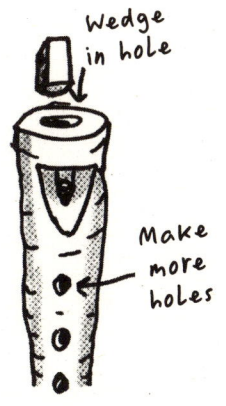

DAY 95

String dot-to-dot

string dot-to-dot doughnut

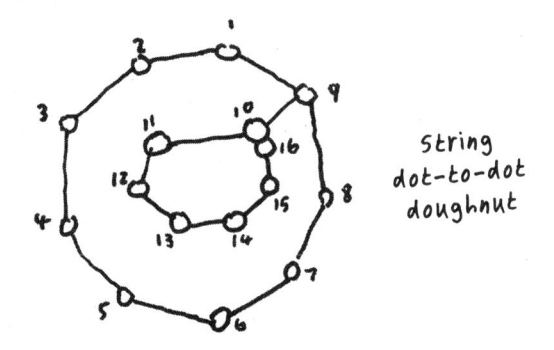

Grab a bag of potatoes.

Work out what design you're going to create for your dot-to-dot. Draw it freehand or trace it from a book or magazine onto a piece of paper first. It'll have to be fairly simple as it's a dot-to-dot!

To find out where to put the dots, place a sheet of tracing paper over the design and trace the dots. When you pick the tracing paper up it'll just have the dots on it. Number the dots. Write the same numbers on the potatoes.

Now, go into the garden.

Place the potatoes so that when viewed from above – ideally from your bedroom window – you can see your design. Then give your friend/sister/cat a ball of string or wool and tell them to "join the potatoes with the string".

They'll probably be able to work out what your design is as they do it, but if not, invite them upstairs to look out of the window, when all will be revealed!

Suggested designs:

* Smiley face
* Dog
* Cat
* Poo emoji
* Professor Brian Cox
* Doughnut

Make sure you gather up your potatoes at the end – just give 'em a wash and they're as good as new!

DAY 96

Declare your independence!

Tired of having to obey THEIR rules? Why not declare your bedroom an independent state? Give this new country a name like Bedroomville, or Bedistan or the United States of My Bedroom.

Next time your mum or dad says, "Your bedroom is such a state!", say, "Yes, actually it's an independent state! Where's your passport?!"

Create your own list of laws: a minimum pocket money allowance set by YOU, free sweets to the under-18s, lower the driving age to 12, bedtime to be decided by a committee that you appoint. This can be an ongoing process – just add new laws as they occur to you.

Make yourself the president or king/queen. Appoint other people (friends, siblings) to key positions of power in your new country, such as prime minister and chancellor of the exchequer. Design new passports and issue them to those you think are worthy of citizenship.

DAY 97

Set up your infrastructure!

Let me lick the back of your head!

← The stamp

Design new coins and banknotes, stamps, driving licences and ID cards for Bedroomville.

Like most countries, you'll need your own police force and army too, so you'd better design their uniforms too.

There's a lot to do when you run a country!

DAY 98

Let your free flag fly

Design a flag for your new country. Take a look at some flags from other countries to see how they tackled it.

When you've designed it, draw it out, paint in the colours and stick it on your bedroom door. Underneath it, write "Welcome to [INSERT NAME OF NEW COUNTRY HERE]".

← The flag

SILLY FACT NUMBER 10

Underarm hair – like your dad's got – actually starts on the top of his head and migrates down to the underarm area at night. This is why he has less hair on his head the older he gets and yet he can't now flatten his arms to his sides due to the bulky underarm hair (yuck).

DAY 99
Write a new national anthem

Adopt a new national anthem for your new country, or take the existing national anthem and change the words, like I have…

God Save Harry Hill

(sung to tune of "God Save the King")

God save our Harry Hill!
President of Bedroomville!
God save H. Hill!

Da na nan-na!

(Da na nan-na!)
Send him victorious,
Bald and hilarious,
He's not a Sagittarius,
God save Harry Hill.

DAY 100

Come up with your own silly chants

Tired of the same old playground chants? Me too! So let's make up some new ones! If you're stuck for an idea, you can always base it on an existing playground chant.

So, for instance, the one we all know that goes ...

Mickey Mouse, in his house,
Pulling down his trousers.
Quick, Mum, wipe his bum!
O-U-T spells OUT!

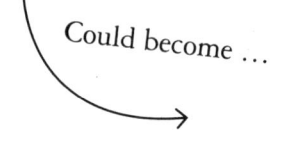

Could become ...

King Charles, in his palace,
Pulling up his pants.
Along came Camilla
And filled them up with ants!
O-U-T spells out!

Or ...

What's the time? Half past nine.
Hang your knickers on the line.
When the postman comes along,
Hurry up and put them on.

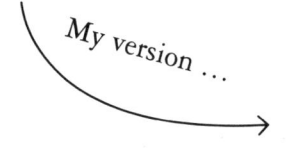

My version ...

What's the time? Half past four.
Hang your knickers on the door.
Sellotape them to your socks
Then post them through the letterbox.

DAY 101

Request a royal visit

Write a letter to the King inviting him round to your recently declared independent bedroom. As a fellow monarch, I'm sure he'll be keen to visit.

DAY 102

Teach your car to wave

Put a glove on the end of each of the windscreen wipers on your mum or dad's car (or see if an aunt, uncle or friendly neighbour will let you tamper with theirs). Next time he or she turns them on: "Hey! What are you waving at, Mr and Mrs Windscreen Wiper?"

DAY 103

Introduce a courgette to a cucumber

Put a courgette in with the cucumbers at the supermarket (well, they look similar) – maybe they could be friends! While you're at the supermarket, buy some flour – you'll need it tomorrow...

Hi, I'm a courgette

And I'm a cucumber.

A BLIND DATE

DAY 104

Create your own muck

Is there a funnier silly practical joke than fake dog muck on your dad's favourite furnishings? If there is, I don't know what it is! Sure, you can buy a plastic joke dog muck from a joke shop, but why waste money and contribute to the build-up of plastics in the world when you can make your own, biodegradable dog muck for next to nothing.

You'll need to make some papier mâché – which I'm sure you know how to make – if not, check out a recipe online.

Once you've got a nice bowl full of mushed-up paper, make some dog muck shapes with your hands. Place them to dry on a wire cooling rack like people use for cakes and put them in the warmest place you can find – in an airing cupboard, out in the sun or, if someone's just used the oven and it's SWITCHED OFF, ask an adult whether you can put your rack of muck in as it cools down.

Depending on how warm it is, it might take a couple of days for them to dry out completely. The thicker you make your muck, the longer it will take – so bear that in mind when you're making them.

Once they're dry, paint them muck-coloured with whatever paint you can get your hands on – brown obviously, but you might like to add some other colours too. (Yuck! I'm beginning to feel a bit sick.)

Here are some suggested shapes:

Some dog muck shapes for you to try

- The love heart
- The dollop
- The UFO
- The leaf
- The top hat
- The teardrop
- The hot cross bun
- The horseshoe

Then place your dog muck where it's going to annoy your parents/teachers/shopkeeper the most – e.g., the sofa, the bedroom carpet, your parents' bed (especially the pillow!), the stairs, the gym.

If you don't have a dog, a cat might work, but it might be better to find a friend who has got one and plant your muck in their house. Or if you've got your nan staying, you could try blaming her!

DAY 105

Play Egg Smash!

Take six eggs – get your pet adult to hard-boil five of them, leaving one uncooked, fresh and nice and runny.

Put the eggs in a bowl – taking care not to break them (which will give it away) – then, with a couple of friends, take it in turns to wear a blindfold. Or, if you really trust each other, just close your eyes and pick an egg.*

After a count of 1–2–3, smash the egg on your forehead. If it's a hard-boiled one, there'll be very little mess, but if it's the fresh one, there'll be carnage! Do it outside on a fine day – and I'd suggest you wear an apron.

* I'm afraid this is not the game for you if you are allergic to eggs, but don't worry, there are plenty more silly activities to choose from.

DAY 106

Create your own silly superhero

As much as I like Superman, Spider-Man and Wonder Woman, THEY'RE QUITE SERIOUS, AREN'T THEY? Surely there's room for a silly superhero?

I'd like you to come up with one.

Think about what your superhero's super power would be.

Maybe it's Flat-Pack-Furniture-Man, who, instead of fingers, has different-sized Allen keys, screwdrivers and spanners. When he hears of someone struggling to put up some flat-pack furniture, he runs to the rescue and helps them out.

Or Super-Silly-Dancer Person, who turns up if someone's looking a bit fed up and does a silly dance to cheer them up.

My silly superhero is BICCY-MAN.

When Biccy-Man sees someone with a cup of tea but no biscuit, he arrives with a choice of Bourbons or custard creams. Biccy-Man to the rescue!

DAY 107

Design a superhero outfit

Once you've settled on a name for your silly superhero, design an outfit for him or her.

Giant biscuit

Mask to hide Biccy-Man's true identity

Clean pants

Tights

IT'S BICCY-MAN!

Did someone say "pants"?

Bring your superhero to life

Make your silly superhero outfit as best you can, dress up as your new superhero and get superhero-ing!

Learn to fly

In your superhero outfit, lie on top of a stool. Get a friend to aim an electric fan at you. When filmed from a certain angle (which you can only really find when you're doing it), it looks like you're flying!

"LOOK - I'M FLYING!"

Day 110

I don't like puppets.

Make your own celebrity puppets

We all love puppets, right? Whaddya mean, "No! I hate puppets, Harry!"? Maybe you're mixing with the wrong sort of puppets. The puppets I'm talking about are really, really, really cool cos they feature the latest cool celebs.

SIMON COWELL Puppet

WILL.I.AM PUPPET

FIONA BRUCE PUPPET

You'll need some paper bags. The best ones are those longish white ones that you get in some shops. If you can't get paper bags, you can always make them, but it's a bit of a faff. Or, I suppose, you might be able to buy them. Divide each paper bag up into thirds: the top third will be the puppet's head and the bottom two thirds will be its body. Now, find a photo of the celebrity you're planning to puppetize and copy it onto the paper bag. Or you could cut out a celebrity face from a magazine.

Paper triangles for ears →

Rita Ora puppet

Harry Hill puppet

Stouffer puppet

Adrian Serious puppet

Decide what your celebrity is wearing. Draw it on and colour in your puppet with paint, crayons, felt-tips – whatever you have to hand.

If you're feeling really fancy, you could glue fabric onto the paper bag for their clothes. You could jazz it up with sequins or feathers, depending on who you're making.

Then simply place the puppet bag over your hand and watch it come to life! You'll need to make an effort to learn the celeb's voice too.

If you don't like the idea of celebrity puppets, you could make them of anyone you like: your teachers, your friends and family – even your pets. The world is your oyster.*

* Not sure why people say "the world is your oyster" because I got very ill after I ate one.

I don't like it!

DAY 111

Create a puppet TV

Get hold of a cardboard box* – the largest you can find, ideally XXL. I know what you're thinking: "Where are we supposed to get all this cardboard, Harry?!" Well, try and persuade your mum to buy a bulky electronic item from the local superstore, or you could try taking a trip out to the superstore and ask whether they have any spare cardboard boxes lying around out the back.

A cardboard box

A SLIGHTLY longer cardboard box

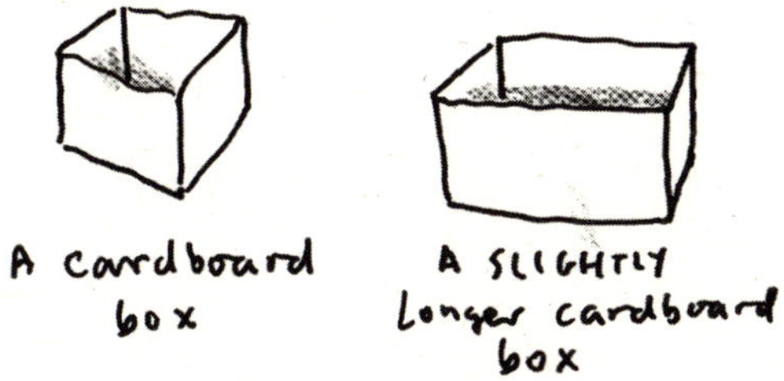

Show them this note – it should help: ⟶

(If you can't get a big cardboard box, you could always skip this day and come back to it when you have one.)

ANYWAY…

Dear Manager of Superstore,
Re: Strange Child in Your Shop
Please provide my friend with any spare cardboard boxes you might have lying around out the back. Rest assured they will be put to a very silly use.
Yours since-silly,
Harry Hill x
President — The Royal Order of Upside-Down Snow Ferrets

* Yes! Another one! I did warn you you'd need a lot of cardboard…

Take the cardboard box and cut a window in it – approximately 60 cm wide by 90 cm long – it doesn't have to be that long ... it's just got to look like a telly.

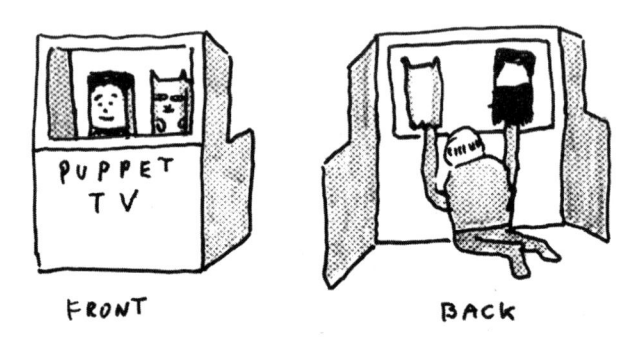

FRONT

BACK

Decorate the front bit of it to look like a TV by painting round the hole – or frame – black. You are now ready to put on your first programme...

Why are you still Reading This Book?!

UH-OH! ADRIAN is back.

Put on your celebrity puppet TV show

It's time to put your celebrity paper bag puppets to work by putting on a puppet TV show with them. The sillier the show, the better. Invite family and friends to watch – you could even charge them for tickets!

You'll need a script, but don't let that put you off – it can be pretty loose. If you're stuck for a story, you could always try basing it on an existing show that features a lot of celebrities – like one of the many reality TV shows or a celebrity quiz show like *Catchphrase, Pointless, The Chase* or *Panorama*. Or cast a pantomime with as many of your favourite celebrities as you want. Why not do *Cinderella*, with Ariana Grande playing Cinders, Harry Styles as Buttons and Boris Johnson and Donald Trump as the ugly sisters?

SIMON COWELL Puppet

WILLIAM PUPPET

FIONA BRUCE PUPPET

Or you could try recreating a scene from your favourite film. Whatever show you're putting on, think about the whole experience:

* **Tickets** – design and make your own tickets.

* **Souvenir brochure** – this is your chance to give the audience a little bit of information about your show before it starts.

* **Snacks** – popcorn is quick and easy to make – and it'll put everyone in a good mood for the show.

* **Music** – as the audience are taking their seats, put them in a good mood by playing their favourite tunes.

* **Pre-show announcements** – ramp up the excitement by making announcements like: "No flash photography or filming during the show", "Latecomers will not be admitted" and "Please take your seats. Tonight's performance of [insert name of show here] will start in five minutes…"

My main advice is: KEEP IT SHORT! No one ever complains that a show is too short, but everyone moans about a show that's too long.

DAY 113

Turn nothing into something

Turn these shapes into silly creatures or objects.

That gives me an idea!

DAY 114

Stage an invasion of the cucumbers

Make a big fuss to your mum and dad/carers/parole officer about hearing that there have been reports of genetically modified cucumbers escaping from the new (but secret!) hydroponic vegetable factory that's opened up near "the ring road". Tell them that the local people are calling it "an invasion of the cucumbers"!

Pop a cucumber on the doorstep, ring the front doorbell and … HIDE. Watch from a safe distance as your adult tries to understand how the cucumber got there. If you really want to go for it, you could hide a smart speaker in a box next to the cucumber and make it look like the cucumber is saying, "I am a cucumber! Take me to your leader!" Or record a fake news bulletin warning of the invasion and make it look like it's coming from the radio.

Maybe you can think of some other silly stuff you could do to make people believe there's an actual cucumber takeover in progress!

DAY 115

Make a hammock for a smiley potato

Make a hammock for a smiley potato from one of those face masks we all wore during the Covid pandemic, then hang it in a tree or a bush.

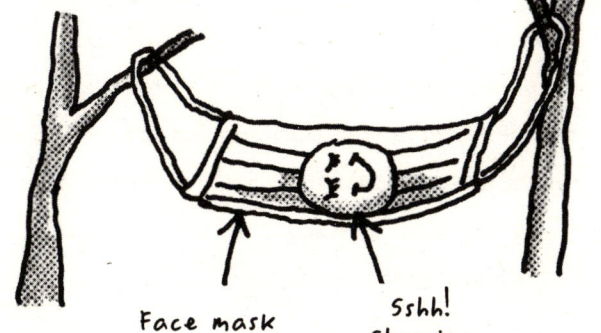

Face mask

Sshh! Sleeping potato

DAY 116

Become a silly poet

I wandered lonely as a ... trowel? ... shroud...? Er ... Lovely dog ... er...

Poetry is HARD!

Ever heard of a limerick? No, it's not a spicy black sweet – you're thinking of liquorice! A limerick is a five-line poem where the first, second and fifth lines rhyme with each other and the third and fourth rhyme with each other – the easiest way is to give you a few examples:

There once was a lady from Leeds,
Who swallowed a packet of seeds.
It soon came to pass
She was covered with grass
And has all the tomatoes she needs.

There was a young farmer from Crete,
Who was so exceedingly neat.
When he got out of bed,
He stood on his head,
To make sure of not soiling his feet.

The incredible Wizard of Oz
Retired from his business because
He was caught in a blizzard,
Which upset the poor wizard,
So he wasn't the wizard he was.

A tutor who taught me the flute
Tried to teach two young tooters to toot.
Said the two to the tutor,
"Is it harder to toot, or …
To tutor two tooters to toot?"

Why not try to write your own limerick? If it helps, you could base it in the town you're from.

DAY 117

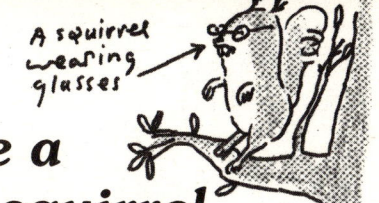

Become a pen pal to a squirrel

A squirrel wearing glasses

Write a note to a squirrel and leave it where squirrels tend to hang out – you know, trees. See if the squirrel replies. Keep writing to him. Maybe he needs glasses or a pen and paper? Provide these next time you leave a letter for him.

> Dear Squirrel,
> How are you? How are the family? I'm fine, although mum has had a cough recently. Here's a picture of an acorn.
> Best wishes
> Harry
> ps Please write back.

DAY 118

Make some water music

Fill a recorder full of water and start blowing. If anyone asks what you're playing, say "Handel's Water Music"!

If you're not able to fill it with water, lower the end of a recorder into a bowl of water and play!

If you can't get a recorder, a kazoo will do ... or even a whistle.

Day 119

Help an ant day

I'm sure ants are pretty fed up with people walking all over their nests. The problem is that ants' nests are often difficult to see, which is why I'm suggesting we give them a little bit of help, and make small signs to warn people away.

Cut out some small rectangles of paper – about the size of a postage stamp – and write your warning messages on them in black felt-tip: things like: "PRIVATE PROPERTY OF THE ANTS! KEEP OFF!" and "TRESPASSERS WILL BE BITTEN!" and "WALK CAREFULLY PAST THIS ANTS' NEST!"

Tape your sign to a twig or a cocktail stick and stick it in the ground next to the ants' nest.* Well done, you've done your bit to help the ants and the rest is up to them.

To any ants reading this: maybe build the nests further away from where people are walking? Just an idea.

* Ants can be a bit bitey, so be careful not to disturb their nest.

DAY 120

You made it!

CONGRATULATIONS! YOU'RE NOW 0.328767123287671 OF THE WAY THROUGH THIS BOOK, WHICH MEANS YOU'VE ONLY GOT 0.671232876712329 OF THE BOOK LEFT!

SO, TAKE THE DAY OFF! Watch some telly! Read a book! Annoy your brother! We'll see you tomorrow!

DAY 121

Create your own cartoon characters

Make up and draw a new set of cartoon characters that no one has ever seen before! They could be based on your favourite animals, or your schoolteachers, or your group of friends, or even some people or animals that you've seen on TV.

STOUFFER POTATO

Mr Smiley Potato

MRS SMILEY POTATO

BABY SMILEY POTATO

DAY 122

Give your cartoon characters something to do

Draw a comic strip based on your new cartoon characters. Coming up with a title first might help – maybe your characters are based on your smiley potatoes, so how about: "The Smiley Potatoes Meet the King", "The Smiley Potatoes Go on Holiday" or "The Smiley Potatoes Enter *Britain's Got Talent*".

It's probably best to jot down a simple story first – and make sure you've got a good strong funny ending.

DAY 123

Bring your cartoon characters to life

Make your new set of cartoon characters out of modelling clay or, if you can't get any of that, use papier mâché, or worst-case scenario ... mud.

Day 124

Give a home to a feather

Pick a feather! Any feather you like – preferably one with plenty of personality. Birds occasionally drop their feathers – if you ask nicely – after all, they've got loads of them! Or you can pick one out of a pillow or pinch one from a feather duster.

Get to know your feather. Give him or her a name. I call my feather "Frankie Frankenfeather".

Make a little house for your feather out of a matchbox. Take your feather with you on trips to the cinema, zoo or when you go and visit friends. Waft your feather around the garden with a piece of cardboard to keep it fit.

come back, Frankie!

Result of too much wafting

day 125

That's what you look like

Draw eight funny faces on a piece of card, or cut out some faces from magazines and alter them with a marker pen. Give them wrinkles, eye bags or black eyes; black out some of their teeth; colour their hair green – you know, make them look really VERY ATTRACTIVE!!!

That's what you look like!

1. Stick them on a circle of card approximately the size of a small plate so you end up with a kind of wheel of faces.

2. Cut a hole in the middle of the card, just big enough for you to get your index finger through.

3. Take your wheel of faces, stick it on the end of your finger and go up to someone and ask them their first name.

4. Spell out their name moving the wheel round one face for each letter. Then ask them their favourite colour.

5. Move the wheel back the other way, one face per letter. Finally, ask them what their favourite animal is (to be honest, it doesn't really matter what questions you ask – you could ask them what their favourite TV programme is or their favourite meal from Nando's – it's really just about moving the wheel).

6. Each time, move the wheel the opposite way one face per letter. When you get to the final letter, point to the face you've landed on and say, "You see that? That's what you look like!"

I DON'T LIKE THIS! ← A. SERIOUS

DAY 126

Clean the car

Clean the family car with a toothbrush.

I've never been outside before!

A TOOTHBRUSH

> **You'll need:**
> * A bucket of soapy water
> * A toothbrush
> * Quite a lot of TIME!!!

If you haven't got a car, clean your bike instead. If you haven't got a bike, then clean your flip-flops. If you haven't got a pair of flip-flops, just clean your teeth!

DAY 127

Caption competition

Try adding a caption and maybe some speech bubbles to a photograph you see in a magazine or paper. It could just be a conversation between two dogs.

Hi!

Sorry, I don't speak Dog.

DAY 128

Make up a smiley potato rap

Remember the smiley potatoes from **Day 29**? Wonder what they're up to now? Well, why not write a rap about them? What do you mean, there aren't many words that rhyme with "potato"?! You can use someone else's beats, but the words should be your own. Here's my attempt:

Smiley Potato Rap

Yo! Everybody wanna say hello
To a guy with a face like a ball of dough?
Mysterious like Vincent Van Gogh!
Say his name, it's Smiley Potato!
Yo, Smiley! Tell me, did you stub your toe*
On a chair in the bedroom of your château?
Or possibly on your trip to Mexico?
Smiley, are you comin' to the show?
Then maybe have a slice of chocolate gateau,
On the patio,
In the afterglow.
Then kiss another spud under the mistletoe
And knock her down like a domino,
Cos your breath smelled a lot like a tomato.
Who else you been kissing, Mr Smiley Potato?

It's really good, right? I'd love to hear what you come up with!

* OK, potatoes don't actually have toes — it's called POETIC LICENCE, OK?????

> **SILLY FACT NUMBER 13**
> The Highway Code was originally developed as a way of talking about roads in a secret way that other people wouldn't understand.

DAY 129

Start a silly collection

Some people spend their life collecting stamps or theatre tickets or matchbox covers – which, frankly, is pretty silly – so why not start a silly collection of your own? You could collect anything from the tiny stickers you get on fruit to favourite barcodes, jam labels, lolly wrappers, the little spoons you get in tubs of ice cream – anything you can stick in your scrapbook.

Make sure you label each item with where you found it and the date. It's surprising how satisfying making a collection of something is! You never know ... one day it might be worth something.*

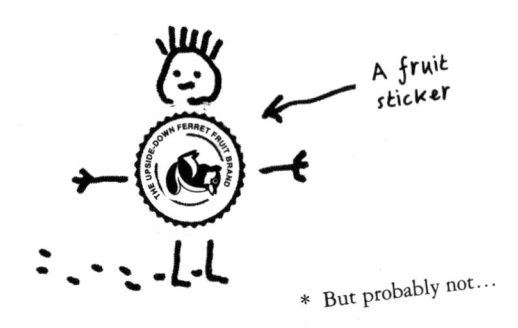

* But probably not...

DAY 130

Hold a sunflower race

Plant five sunflower seeds in a row against a fence. If you haven't got space in your garden, or if you don't have a garden, plant them in a window box or even a Tupperware container filled with earth (put some holes in the bottom of the container, though, so the water can drain out).

Measure 60 cm (the height of two rulers) above where you've planted them, then string a ribbon across with a couple of drawing pins. Write "FINISH LINE" on the ribbon.

Now the race is on! The first sunflower to pass the finish line wins!

DAY 131

Ventriloquism day

Spend the day talking without moving your lips. Maybe spend the first hour of the day practising in the mirror. Tricky words to say with your mouth closed are words with a "B" or a "P" in, so bear that in mind. When someone asks you what you'd like for lunch, don't say "a buttered brown bap and a Bath bun", say "a cheese croissant and a yoghurt"!

I HATE! ventriloquism — and I said that *without* moving my lips!

UH-OH! It's ADRIAN SERIOUS AGAIN!

DAY 132

Give your knees a personality

Draw faces on your knees (use washable pens please!) and, by twitching your kneecaps, watch them come to life.

Hi! Hi!

DAY 133

Stage an alien invasion

It's not cucumbers this time,* it's the real thing: actual aliens!!!

Draw the top half of an alien on the biggest piece of cardboard you can find – just the head and shoulders will do. It's up to you what your alien looks like, but in my experience, most aliens are green, have large heads, big black eyes and narrow slits for their noses and mouths. You might like to give yours three eyes and four mouths – or even TWO HEADS!!!

Paint the alien whatever colours you like (or have left!). Cut your alien out and stick him or her looking out of your bedroom window.

This will stop actual aliens from trying to get into your house as they'll realize that you've already been visited.

---

* See Day 114: Stage an invasion of the cucumbers.

DAY 134

Make your own UFSO

Make a UFSO or Unidentified Flying Silly Object by drawing round a couple of dinner plates onto white paper and cutting the circles out. Glue or tape the edges together, leaving a gap of maybe 15 cm that you can then get some stuffing in. Bubble wrap makes good stuffing, or kitchen roll (which will help you get closer to that inner cardboard tube!)

Cover the whole thing with tin foil. If you're feeling really energetic, you could stick or paint on some details like windows, maybe with an alien waving.

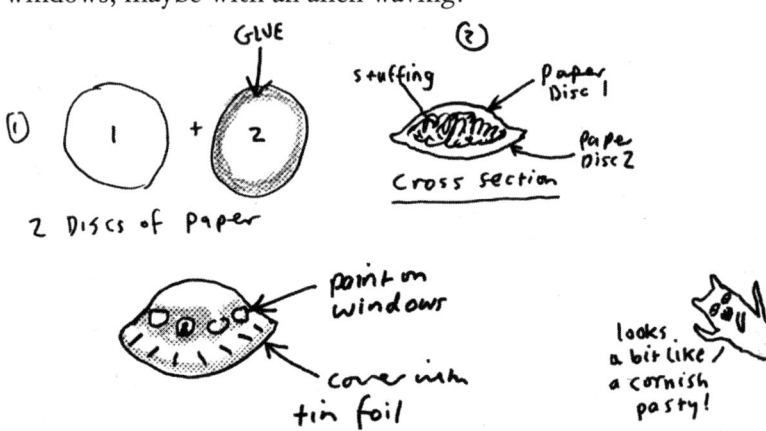

Once you're happy with your interplanetary craft, go outside and throw your flying saucer up into the air.

Take a photograph of it – preferably against an empty sky so it's harder to work out how big it is. Then show the photo to your friends and say casually, "Got visited by aliens yesterday, just saying…"

DAY 135

Design a silly hotel complex

I love a nice hotel, don't you? There's a choice of swimming pools, a kids' play area, a kids' club, several restaurants to choose from and a huge breakfast buffet every morning.* There's even a shuttle bus to take you into the local village, where often they don't sell anything you really want, but you buy something anyway – well, you ARE on holiday!

So today you're going to design your own silly hotel complex. Give it a name – something like "Hotelly World Resort" or "Silly View Hotel". Think about some of the services the hotel might offer and some of the themed rooms that might be available, the restaurants, the gym, the pools, a ballroom, a conference centre – give them all a silly twist!

THE SILLY VIEW HOTEL AND ALL-IN RESORT

*I love the breakfast buffet! Most mornings I'll have muesli, toast, a croissant and jam, full fry-up, including beans and hash browns and a sausage, then I'll have a yoghurt, some churros, a few slices of smoked salmon, ham and soft cheese, and then I'll wash it all down with a bright purple Slush Puppie!

DAY 136

Design a logo

Design a logo for your silly hotel.

DAY 137

Swing on a gate

Swing on a gate. That's it!
As you're doing it, say,
"Weeeeeeeeeeeeee!"

SILLY PEOPLE FROM HISTORY NUMBER 5: GERALD TYRWHITT-WILSON

Gerald (1883–1950) regularly had afternoon tea with his pet giraffe.

DAY 138

Make a raft for a bee

We've all seen bees struggling to stay afloat in ponds, puddles and swimming pools. They've obviously thought, "I'd like to cool down in that water" then forgotten that they're not very good at swimming. Everyone knows that there's a shortage of bees and that we need them to pollinate our flowers and fruit trees and crops, so it's really important that we try and save these silly bees who have got themselves in a bit of a watery pickle.

The raft doesn't have to be that big – this isn't a pleasure cruise; we're just saving one bee. I reckon it needs to be 5–8 cm. I always use twigs that I've stuck together with modelling glue. I suggest you write "BEE RAFT" on it just in case they do speak English. (With all that buzzing, they sound kind of French to me, right? So maybe write it in French too. "Bee raft" in French is *Radeau d'abeille*.)

Attach a piece of string to your raft and float it out towards the drowning bee. Once the bee has climbed onto the raft, you can pull it in to the safety of dry land.* Leave the bee on the raft in the sun to dry out and reflect on its mistake. Hopefully, it will be fine. If not, you did your best – see **Day 30: Hold a funeral for a fly** to give it a good send-off.

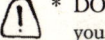

> * **DON'T TOUCH THE BEE** as bees can sting you, which is incredibly ungrateful.

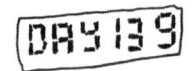

Make a silly fancy-dress outfit

Here's a very silly (and cheap!) fancy-dress outfit.

> **You'll need:**
> * A newspaper or two
> * PVA glue
> * A pair of scissors

What to do:

Take your newspaper and glue the edges of some sheets together to make four much larger sheets. Once the glue is dry, lay some of your clothes – trousers, T-shirts, skirts – on top of two of the large sheets and draw around them, leaving a good couple of centimetres around the edges. Cut them out, place them on top of the two remaining sheets, draw round these and cut them out so that you've got two copies.

Glue the edges of the copies together, except where there should be gaps: for instance, the neck, armholes and the bottom of a shirt, and the waist and bottoms of the trousers.

Once the glue is dry, your clothes are prêt-à-porter! (That's French for "ready to wear".) You might also like to wear a newspaper hat and maybe cover an old pair of shoes with some spare bits of newspaper.

You don't really have to have a reason to wear your new newspaper clothes, but if it's for a fancy-dress day, just say you're going as "The News". The other great thing about this outfit is that if it rains you've got instant papier mâché!*

DAY 140
Attack yourself with your own hand

This one is easier to demonstrate than describe, but here goes...

Stand in a doorway with your right side against the door frame. Bring your right hand in from behind the door frame and round your neck – to anyone standing in front of the doorway it looks like someone else's hand is attempting to strangle you.

* See Day 104: Create your own muck.

DAY 141

Go fishing in a puddle

This is a great thing to do on a rainy day! You don't need a fancy fishing rod, just a long-ish stick and some string – and instead of a fish hook, use a safety pin. For bait, use a piece of bread that you've mushed up into a ball.

Take a bucket just in case you catch a fish – and while you're waiting for something to bite, you can turn the bucket upside down and sit on it. If you're worried you might not catch anything, draw a picture of a fish and colour it in with felt-tips, or cut out a picture from a magazine or print one off.

Cut out your fish and attach it to your "hook". When someone walks past, pull the fish out of the puddle and cry, "I caught one!" The next thing you know, they'll be sitting next to you trying to catch one for themselves!

DAY 142

Pretend someone's stuck in a post box

Next time you and a friend are walking past a post box, look into the slit in the post box and say in a very loud voice, "What do you mean, you're stuck? Well, how did you get in there in the first place?" If your friend asks you what is going on, tell them, "My little sister got stuck in the post box!"

Obviously if they start to call for the fire brigade to rescue them, you'd better confess that you're just being silly. If they start to get a bit angry, just show them this message.

THAT NORMALLY FIXES IT!

Hi there,

Sorry about the post box thing, but it's my fault: I told them to do it. I promise I'll buy you an ice cream next time I see you.

Luv 'n' stuff,

Harry Hill x

President – The Royal Order of Upside-Down Snow Ferrets

Make a silly fortune-teller

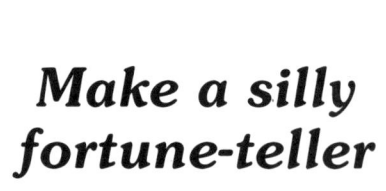

DAY 143

You may have seen one of these before – but not like this! Take a piece of square paper – or convert a regular A4 piece of paper into a square piece of paper. Then fold it as per this diagram:

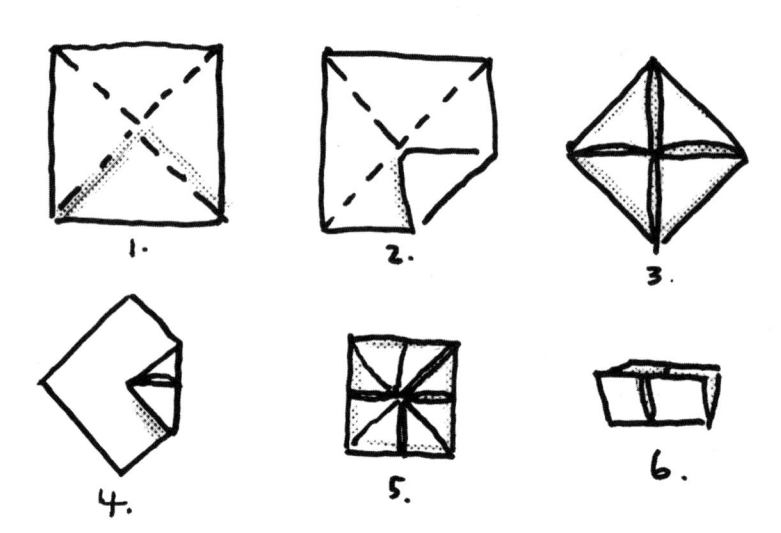

* Write numbers on the eight triangles.
* Draw four animals on the top of the fortune-teller.
* Open up the triangles labelled 1 and 2 and write your silly predictions underneath each number. Repeat this for each numbered flap, so you have eight different predictions. Close the flaps once you've written all the fortunes.

* Slide your fingers underneath the squares to operate it. Ask a friend to choose an animal and spell it out letter by letter. So, if it's a badger it's B-A-D-G-E-R. As you do so, move your fingers with each letter, opening and closing the fortune-teller. Then get your friend to pick a number and count it out in a similar way.

* Last, have them pick another number to reveal their fortune. Lift that flap and read what it says.

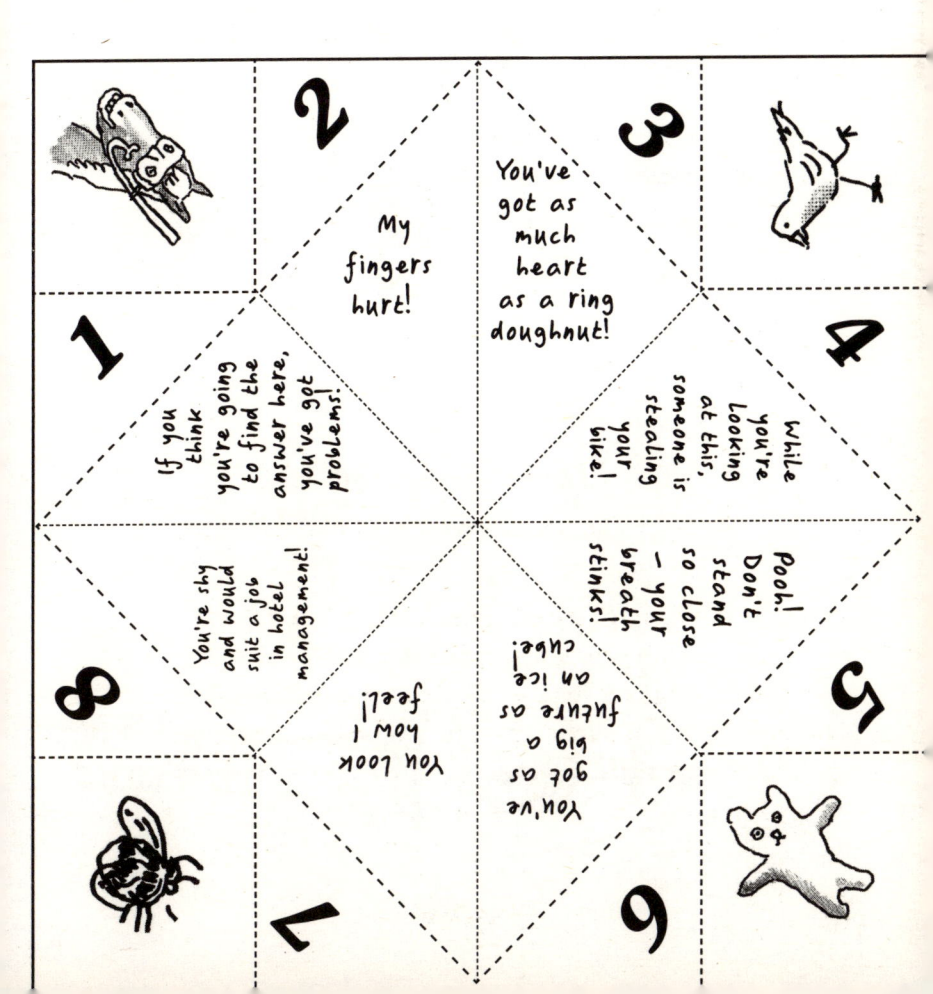

2 — My fingers hurt!

3 — You've got as much heart as a ring doughnut!

1 — If you think you're going to find the answer here, you've got problems!

4 — While you're looking at this, someone is stealing your bike!

8 — You're shy and would suit a job in hotel management!

5 — Pooh! Don't stand so close — your breath stinks!

7 — You look how I feel!

6 — You've got as big a future as an ice cube!

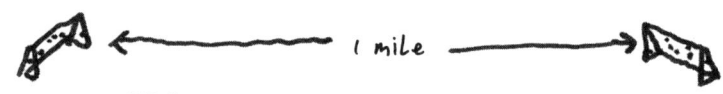

DAY 144 — Play a game of long way away football

Arrange a football match, but put the two goals as far away as possible – ideally so far that the goalkeepers can't even see each other, like maybe a mile away. Now play football. Fun, right?

DAY 145 — Hug something silly

Some people like to hug trees. What's the silliest thing you've ever hugged? Try hugging a tree to start with, then maybe a bush or a lamppost, then progress on to parking ticket machines, phone boxes and washing machines. If you can, take photographs of all the different things you've hugged and stick them in your silly scrapbook.

HEY! THAT'S MY TREE!

ADRIAN SERIOUS

DAY 146

Make a car journey quite interesting

Car journeys can be SO boring, can't they? Your pet adult is either listening to THEIR music – someone called Charles Aznavour, or The Prodigy – or they're tuned into something called Radio 4, which seems to have been designed solely to bore young people to death!*

If you complain, they tell you to "look out of the window and enjoy the lovely scenery" or say, "Let's play I-Spy." You know, "I spy with my little eye…" I mean, really. I wouldn't mind, but I don't have a little eye – I've got two eyes of larger-than-average size for my age.

I love I-Spy!

So what's the answer?

Well, try playing the pub sign story game! Make up a story inspired by the names of pubs that you pass on your way. Like all good stories, it starts with "Once upon a time … there was a [you see a pub called THE KING'S HEAD] king who had a very big head… [You see a pub called THE BEAR TAVERN] Now this king kept a pet bear who loved to dance [you see a pub called THE PRINCE OF WALES] with the Prince of Wales…" And so it goes on until you run out of pubs or you get bored again – at which point everyone in the car says, "And they all lived happily ever after!"

* Otherwise, why would anyone decide to make a drama based on a farm with no pictures to look at to help you work out what's going on?

DAY 147

Make a cardboard surfboard

Today you're going to make a cardboard surfboard.

I know what you're thinking: "Where am I gonna get all that cardboard from?" Well, get your mum (or dad – no stereotypes here! Down with the patriarchy!) to order a new fridge. The fridge will come wrapped in cardboard. Hey presto, you've got enough cardboard for your cardboard surfboard.

"OK," you're saying, "but how do I get them to buy a new fridge?" Well, here are some things you can say to get your mum/guardian/dad/rich benefactor* to buy a new fridge so you can get the free cardboard for your surfboard:

* Complain about the fridge. Say things like: "The fridge isn't very cold, Mum/Guardian/Dad/Rich Benefactor!" or "My friends have been teasing me about how old our fridge is. Can we get a new one, please?"

* Or, if your parents are really gullible: "I've just seen a news flash that said our model of fridge was fitted with artificial intelligence and in the next ten days it will come to life and attack us when we're trying to unload all the shopping."

* But not your auntie cos she just bought you a scrapbook.

How to make your cardboard surfboard:

It's actually really easy – just place a real surfboard onto some cardboard and draw round it, then cut it out. Alternatively, if you haven't got a real surfboard, lie on the cardboard and get a friend or relative to draw round you in a rough surfboard shape. Then cut it out. Hey presto! You now have the basis of your cardboard surfboard.

Now the fun starts… Decorate your cardboard surfboard using poster paints, photos cut from magazines, stuff you've got lying about – like pages from old books by David Walliams – and customize your board.

You might like to add surfing-related slogans like "Surf's Up!", "Everybody's Goin' Surfin'!" or, if you're going surfing on the North Kent coast, "Watch Out for the Sewage!"

Tuck your cardboard surfboard under your arm, head to the duck pond and wait for a big wave (you might have to wave at the ducks first as they're quite shy). Or, as cardboard doesn't do so well in water, head to your kitchen/living room/bedroom and get indoor surfing!

DAY 148

Design a silly cruise ship

Enjoying your holiday?

Not much to do, is there?

Cruise ships these days are amazing, aren't they? They've got discos, theatres, swimming pools, loads of restaurants ... but there's always room for improvement!

Design a silly ship with some of the extras YOU would like to see. How about a zoo or a roller coaster?

DAY 149

Groom a bush

Groom a hedge with a hairbrush. As you're doing this, talk to the bush like a hairdresser does. Say things like: "Going anywhere nice for your holidays this year?" and "Shocking weather we're having!" and "Who brushed your leaves last time – it's a complete mess!"

Skin fade, please!

A BUSH

DAY 150

Release your feather

Remember your feathery pet? No! Not your budgie, the feather you've been looking after since **Day 124**! Today we're going to release your feather back into the wild — a nice way to do this is by throwing the feather out of the window of a moving car. Look out for your feather, though — it's surprising just how often they pop back to say hello.

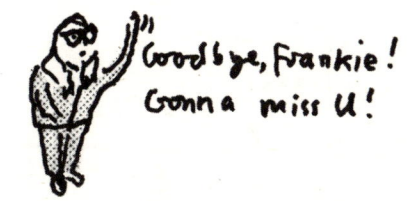

Goodbye, Harry! — I'll be back!

Goodbye, Frankie! Gonna miss U!

Goodbye, Frankie!

SILLY FACT NUMBER 15

The ancient Romans made mosaics because they could only afford to buy very tiny tiles.

How much is this one?

DAY 151

Robot or not?

Take a piece of A4 paper and draw a road junction, complete with traffic lights. Take your time over this and get it as good as you can. Colour in your picture with paints, colouring pencils or felt-tips.

Divide up your picture into a grid of four boxes by four boxes.

Tell your mum, dad or friend that you need to test whether they're a robot or not, then ask them to point at the squares with the traffic lights in! Don't ask me why — it's just really funny!

select all squares with traffic lights

Practise pulling faces

DAY 152

A really important part of being silly is the ability to pull a variety of silly faces, so please get plenty of practice in front of the mirror.

Draw the faces that you pull and give each different face a number, then every time someone mentions a number that you've given to a silly face, pull that silly face. This might happen in a maths lesson, watching the National Lottery or at the deli counter in Sainsbury's. Get your friends to do it too.

DAY 153

Turn a box of cornflakes into a jigsaw puzzle

Get a box of cornflakes and pretend it's a jigsaw puzzle. Empty the cornflakes onto a tray. Study the picture on the front of the box and try to fit the cornflakes together to make the picture.

DAYS 154 AND 155

The biscuit flume

The day has finally arrived when you'll need all those cardboard tubes from toilet rolls and kitchen rolls – which I told you to start saving on **page** 7! – because we're going to make a multi-storey biscuit delivery system or MSBDS for short. It's pretty simple – but highly effective!

Simply tape together all the cardboard rolls you've managed to collect so that you have one long tube. Write on one end "Multi-storey biscuit delivery system IN", and on the other end "Multi-storey biscuit delivery system OUT". Take your MSBDS to the next floor in your house and run it down the stairs, or very carefully stick it out of a gap in a window.

⚠️ PLEASE DON'T OPEN THE WINDOW COMPLETELY OR YOU MIGHT FALL OUT!!!

Tell your mum, friend, neighbour, postman – whoever fancies a biscuit, basically – to position their plate under the tube where it says "OUT". Then pop in the biscuit – I suggest a Bourbon or a custard cream as the larger, round biscuits won't fit and may clog up the system. In a matter of seconds, the person wanting a biscuit will have one.

UNSUITABLE BISCUITS   SUITABLE BISCUITS

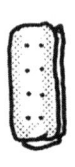

On no account must anyone put their mouth under the tube as the biscuit comes out of the tube with such force that it might knock their front teeth out, or certainly cause them to choke.

The good news is that this system can be used for things other than biscuits. You can write a message and wrap it round a small pebble and drop it down the tube. If you attach a piece of string to the pebble, the person on the other end can write a message for you to pull back up the tube. Maybe you can think of some other uses for the MSBDS?

Here's a video of how to build your flume!

DAY 156

Do a Zoom call headstand

Next time you're on an important business Zoom call – or just having a FaceTime with your nan – put your trousers on your arms and your socks and shoes on your hands and tell whoever's watching that you can do a headstand. Then duck down below the level of the camera and slowly bring your hands (that now look like your feet) up into shot.

To the person on the other end of the call, it'll look like you're doing a headstand.

It doesn't have to be a video call; you could do the same trick from behind the sofa, or below a window to people walking by in the street.

DAY 157

Learn to play the nose flute

Buy a nose flute! It's the silliest instrument you'll ever see! They're only a couple of quid and I swear you'll never look back! Ask an adult to help you attach it to your face with a large rubber band, or some elastic, and off you go! Hours of fun – you can play ANY tune with virtually no musical skill whatever! I repeat: buy a nose flute!!!

Suggested tunes:

* The theme from *Titanic* – "My Heart Will Go On" by Celine Dion
* The theme tune from *Blue Peter*
* Rachmaninoff's Piano Concerto No. 3

DAY 158

Play courgette versus cucumber chequers

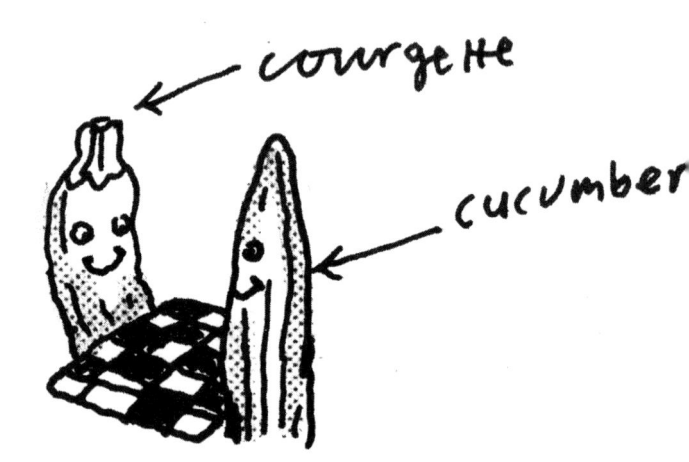

We all enjoy a game of chequers, or draughts, but too often we are stuck without a set to play with, but we do have a courgette and a cucumber rolling around in the bottom of the salad drawer. Here's how you can turn that spare veg into the game you're so looking forward to playing:

* Cut 1 cm-thick slices of cucumber and courgette and place them on a draughts board or chessboard (you'll need 12 slices of each).

* If you don't have a chessboard, get a blank piece of paper, a ruler, a pencil and some black paint or felt-tips and draw an 8x8 grid of squares that are an inch wide. It doesn't have to be exact – you don't really need a ruler, just 64 rough squares. Fill in the bottom left-hand corner in black and then every other square until it looks like a chequerboard.

If you can't get a cucumber or a courgette, you can always use:

- ***Biscuits*** – Bourbons versus custard creams
- ***Sausages*** (cooked, cooled and cut into rounds) – Cumberland versus standard pork
- ***Seafood*** – prawns versus cockles (but these do tend to smell a bit after a while)

DAY 159 Play dead

This works really well after a meal where everyone else is sitting at the table. Lie in the nearest doorway with only your top half showing and announce, "Ladies and gentlemen, a dead body being dragged from a room!"

Then pull yourself out of view with your feet. Weirdly, it looks like you're being dragged off by some sinister person!

DEAD BODY BEING DRAGGED FROM A ROOM TRICK

DAY 160

Make a cake in a hat

This is a cake that requires absolutely no cooking whatsoever! You simply take your dad's hat. Only joking! But you will need a hat that stands up on its own, as opposed to a bobble hat or a baseball cap. The ideal for this is a trilby, so you may have to keep a lookout in the charity shops.

You'll need:

A HAT · CAKE BARS · A RICE KRISPIE · CHOCOLATE SPREAD

INGREDIENTS

Line the inside of the trilby with cling film, then grease with butter. Line with the cake bars, then fill the rest of it up with Rice Krispies and seal the base with chocolate spread.

Invert the trilby onto a plate and, hey presto, your hat cake! Dust a little icing sugar over it to finish it off.

> **Notey-note**
> If you have any allergies, use tasty substitute ingredients for this recipe. Yum!

FINISHED HAT CAKE

(To be honest, it is mainly cake bars.)

Face mask fun

DAY 161

Remember those blue surgical masks we all wore during the Covid pandemic? Chances are you'll probably still have a few lying around. Well, not only do they make excellent hammocks for smiley potatoes, but they can also be used for a very silly visual joke. Take one and make a slit under one of the middle folds.

Put the mask on and arrange it so you can't see the slit, then when you talk the slit opens up to reveal your mouth – I'm not sure why, but it's just really funny!

DAY 162

Interspecies arm wrestling

This silly thing depends on you having a hamster puppet – but it could equally be some other soft toy puppet (see **Day 227**). So, assuming it's a hamster puppet, ask your friend or relative if they think they can beat a hamster at arm wrestling. Most people, unless they're very, very, very weak or very, very, very busy will say "YES!" When they do, say, "OK, prove it!" and produce the hamster puppet on your hand and arm wrestle them with it.

Maybe they've got a puppet they could use too? Make up a league table of all the different species and how good they are at wrestling.

Notey-note

Arm wrestling is meant to be fun, so if it starts hurting, stop!

Become an anti-poet

Make up a limerick that DOESN'T rhyme – or an anti-limerick. Something like…

> *There once was a man called Brian,*
> *Who had an enormous brain.*
> *I know brain doesn't rhyme,*
> *And neither does that…*

Sorry about that – I was in a hurry!

See how people react when you read it out to them.

Pretend it's been snowing in the summer

In the summer, on a nice hot day, put on your warmest coat, a bobble hat, scarf and mittens, then take a spade and go round to your neighbours' house and tell them that you've successfully cleared all the snow from their path.

DAY 165

Make your own mouse basher

Remember the biscuit delivery tube we made on **Day 154**? I hope you didn't throw it away! Today you're going to use it as an extra-long bash-the-mouse game.

Make a mouse however you like – from some fabric glued around a pebble (don't forget the tail!) or a big lump of modelling clay, but remember, it's got to fit easily down a toilet roll tube and it's got to be heavy enough to keep going – we don't want your mouse getting stuck halfway.

You'll need two people for this – one to release the mouse into the top of the tube and the other to stand at the other end of the tube with a rolled-up newspaper ready to bash the mouse as it emerges. It sounds easy, but it's harder than you think. You might want to make several mice so that you don't have to keep going up and down the stairs to fetch them.

Paste any squashed mice into your scrapbook.

Eek!

DAY 166

Use veg as a message system

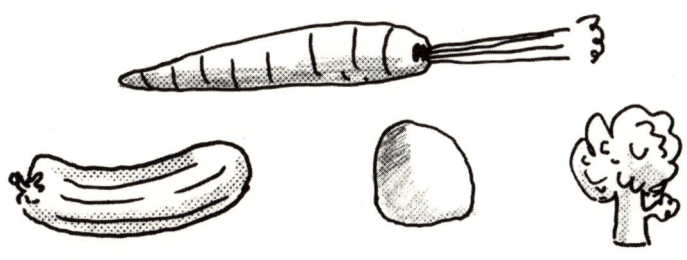

There's no privacy these days, is there? There are scammers hacking into our emails and bank accounts left, right and centre, so it seems that maybe the only real way to ensure complete privacy is to write your messages on bits of paper and smuggle them inside vegetables.

Ask an adult to make a hole in a potato about the size of your finger. Save the piece of potato that came out of the hole with the skin on it – that's going to act as a sort of cork.

Write your message on a thin strip of paper, roll it up and insert it into the hole in your potato. Then block the hole back up with the plug of potato you removed and hand it to the person who the message is for.

Also works with carrots, parsnips and sweet potatoes – but not Brussels sprouts.

When these substances are heated together with a catalyst, they undergo a condensation process whereby water is eliminated and hundreds of molecules become joined together in long chains. Representing the molecules by large and small circles and omitting the water which is formed, we can indicate the change simply as shown in Fig. 32:

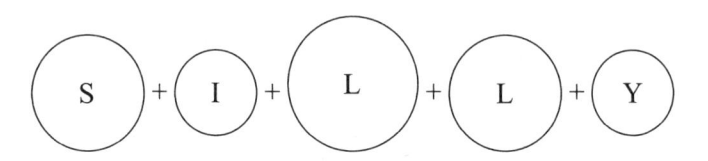

$$\bigcirc S + \bigcirc I + \bigcirc L + \bigcirc L + \bigcirc Y$$

FIG. 32 THE JOINING TOGETHER OF MOLECULES AFTER CONDENSATION

Readers who have a knowledge of the chemical formulae of organic substances may be interested to see the proper chemical equation, which is:

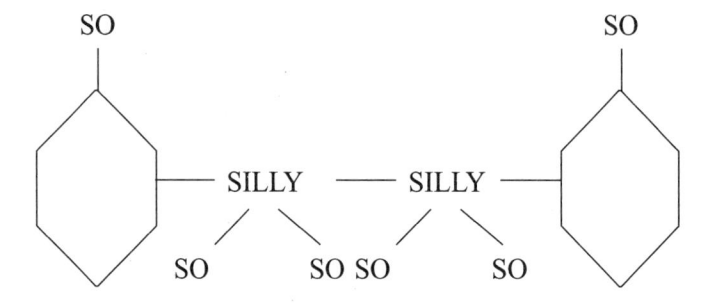

```
    SO                              SO
    |                               |
   /=\                             /=\
  |   |— SILLY — SILLY —          |   |
   \=/    / \      / \             \=/
         SO   SO SO    SO
```

The product is a resinous substance which is dried and ground into a powder. The mixture is fed into a heated steel mould. A hydraulic press is then closed, and in a few seconds, the mixture is pressed to the shape of the mould and at the same time set.

VERY SERIOUS AND NOT SILLY PAGES

When these substances are heated together with a catalyst, they undergo a condensation process whereby water is eliminated and hundreds of molecules become joined together in long chains. Representing the molecules by large and small circles and omitting the water which is formed, we can indicate the change simply as shown in Fig. 32:

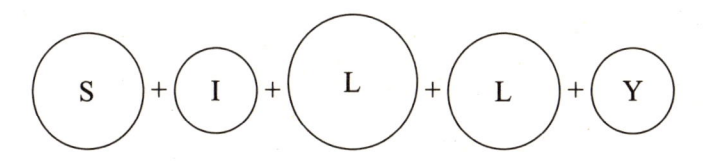

$$\bigcirc S + \bigcirc I + \bigcirc L + \bigcirc L + \bigcirc Y$$

FIG. 32 THE JOINING TOGETHER OF MOLECULES AFTER CONDENSATION

Readers who have a knowledge of the chemical formulae of organic substances may be interested to see the proper chemical equation, which is:

```
         SO                                    SO
          |                                     |
       ⬡ — SILLY — SILLY — ⬡
        / \         / \
      SO   SO SO    SO
```

The product is a resinous substance which is dried and ground into a powder. The mixture is fed into a heated steel mould. A hydraulic press is then closed, and in a few seconds, the mixture is pressed to the shape of the mould and at the same time set.

Make a sponge finger prison

I know this isn't a recipe book, but it's nice occasionally to make something that's silly but also tasty. It also makes a great pudding for your Chicken Tom Jones!*

It's basically a cage made from sponge fingers, which we cement together with whipped cream. The easiest way to explain it is in a song!

The Sponge Finger Prison Song

A sponge finger prison isn't hard to make.
You take some cream, and you give it a shake.
Whip it all up like a big fluffy dream.
Then you take a sponge finger and a blob of cream.
Don't hang about now, don't let it linger,
For to the blob of cream you add another sponge finger!
I hope that you're getting the idea of the scheme,
For to that sponge finger add a blob of cream.
Then you look around for a real dead ringer,
And to the blob of cream, you add another sponge finger!

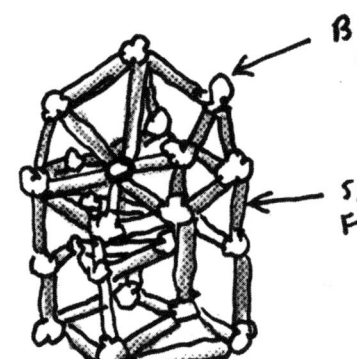

BLOB OF CREAM
SPONGE FINGER

---

* See Day 74: Chicken legend.

Ian the Information Worm

Draw a face on your index finger and ask someone if they've got a question for Ian the Information Worm.

A general knowledge question like: "What is the capital of France?" or "How many legs has Liz Truss got?"

Just before they ask the question, make a fist around your index finger and pop "Ian" up so his face is showing just above your fist.

When they've asked the question, put Ian up to your ear as if he's whispering to you, then say, "Sorry, he doesn't know the answer to that one."

Homemade Happy Families

It's an old game, but you've probably heard of it. Happy Families is where you deal out a special pack of cards made up of various "families" consisting of a mum, a dad, a son and a daughter. The idea is to collect as many whole families as you can.* In the original game it's families like the Grocer family – so it would be Mr Grocer, Mrs Grocer, Master Grocer (the grocer's son) and Miss Grocer (the grocer's daughter). I'm suggesting you make your own set based on your and your friends' families.

You'll need to make about seven families, each with four cards, so that's er ... maths was never my strong point ... I think that's twenty-eight cards.

The easiest way to make the cards is to divide seven sheets of A4 card into four by folding them in half and then half again and cutting them along the fold lines. If you can't get card, use paper and then glue it onto some card – old cereal boxes are good – but use whatever you can find.

Now you've got the blank cards, the fun can start! Either draw pictures of your friends or stick on photographs of them. If there aren't four in their family then just make up a spare brother, sister or whatever! Maybe include their pet dog instead. You might like to include famous families like the Royals, the Kardashians or the Beckhams, or you could make up any family you like.

* Look up the rules of the game online.

Mr Hill	**Mrs Hill**
Master Hill	**Stouffer Hill**

HAVE YOU GOT KIM?

DAY 170

Fingers-in-your-ears Happy Birthday

Sit down at a piano or pick up a guitar or ukulele and tell whoever's birthday it is that you've been learning to play the piano/guitar/ukulele and that you'd like to sing "Happy Birthday" to them. Then, as you sing them the song, just crash your hands up and down on the piano keys, or strum wildly on the guitar or uke. I'm not sure why, but it's very funny!

Check it out here:

SILLY FACT №17

Britain's famous White Cliffs of Dover aren't actually white and should be referred to as the "White Cliffs with Some Brown Bits and Green Stuff on Top of Dover".

Design your own star signs

DAY 171

Last night, as I was trying to get to sleep, I looked up at the stars in the sky and thought to myself, "I must get that hole in the roof fixed!"

But seriously, I do find it very hard to make out how the stars resemble the animals, objects or people they are meant to. Like, for instance, the stars that are supposed to make up Leo the Lion look more like a duck to me!

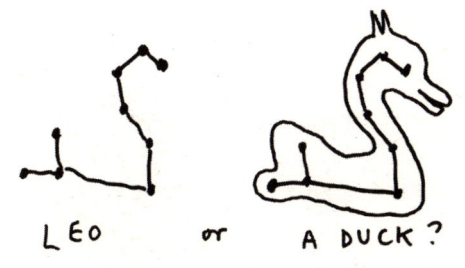

LEO   or   A DUCK?

And to me, the constellation for Pisces looks less like a fish and more like a cat.

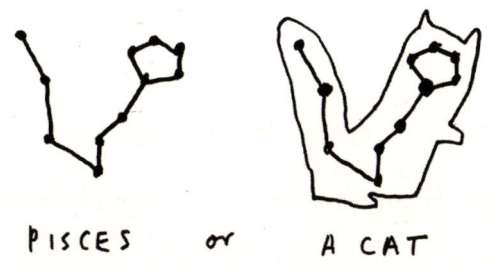

PISCES   or   A CAT

Why not come up with your own star signs? Here are some I thought up:

* The Toilet Brush
* The Micro-Scooter
* The Ford Orion
* The FA Cup

DAY 172

Become a mystic

Write some silly horoscopes for your new star signs.

Here are a few silly ones to start you off...

The Toilet Brush

This week, beware of rogue rubber ducks. They might seem innocent, but their quacks could be hiding a sinister agenda.

The Ford Orion

This week, your spirit animal is a tap-dancing giraffe. Channel its grace and elegance as you navigate social situations. Your lucky number this week is 42, but only if you wear your underwear backwards on Tuesdays.

The Micro-Scooter

This week, Micro-Scooters will discover a hidden talent for interpretive dance inspired by household appliances. Expect a breakthrough performance in the kitchen.

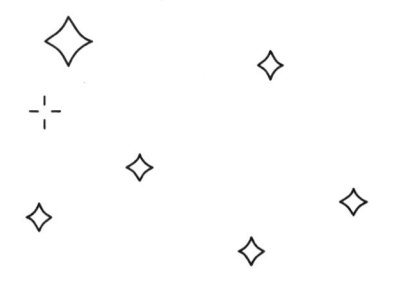

Hi, I'M HORACE COPE AND I CAN SEE INTO THE FUTURE!

DAY 173

The great sock mystery

Gather all the mismatched socks you can find and have a sock detective day. Create "missing sock" posters with rewards for their safe return. Then, organize a sock line-up and interrogate each sock to find out where their partner disappeared to.

DAY 174

Start your own language

Agree with a friend or sibling to substitute some words for other words. So, for instance, say "sausage" instead of "hello" and "flubbywuff" instead of "goodbye". Before you know it, you'll have your own language. This is exactly how French started!

DAY 175

Hold a crab race

Next time you're on a sandy beach, stage a crab race (if you already staged a snail race earlier in the year, then it's pretty much the same, only swap snails for crabs).

Find some crabs by the shore or under a rock in a rock pool – you only need three to make a good race, two if you're pushed; it doesn't really work with one crab. Carefully put them into a bucket.

Draw a circle in the sand, gently turn the bucket over in the centre and, when someone shouts "GO!", lift the bucket and watch 'em run. First crab to cross the circle wins a holiday for two in Aberystwyth. Make sure you put the crabs back where you found them.

Notey-note

Crabs have sharp/pinchy claws, so ask an adult to help you with this activity.

DAY 176

Stage a Silly Olympics

Four years seems a long time to wait between watching the TV show *The Olympics*. I don't understand why it isn't every year; after all, it always gets great TV ratings. How about filling the gaps with "The Silly Olympics" or "The Sillympics", where all the events are, well, silly! Events like...

* The 100 m hop
* The spitathlon (seeing how far you can spit an orange pip)
* The 20 m land swimming
* The flinging-a-sausage-into-a-tree-a-thon

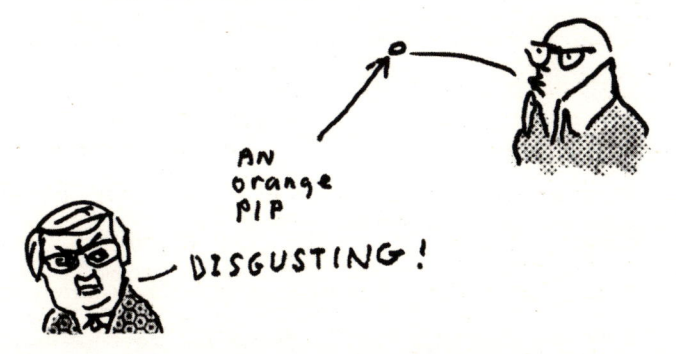

AN orange PIP — DISGUSTING!

That's not enough for a whole two weeks, so help me out – come up with your own silly events, and let's do this thing!!!

DAY 177

Make a fish that spits water

Paint a picture of a fish on a nice big piece of paper, then stick it onto a piece of cardboard. You might like to cut out some strips of cardboard and make a frame for it too. Cut a tiny hole in the mouth just big enough for the nozzle of a water pistol.

Using parcel tape, attach your water pistol to the back of the painting.

Go up to your mum or your friend and ask them whether they think your picture of a fish is very realistic. Say "Go on, take a closer look…" and, when they get within spitting distance, let 'em have it with the water pistol!

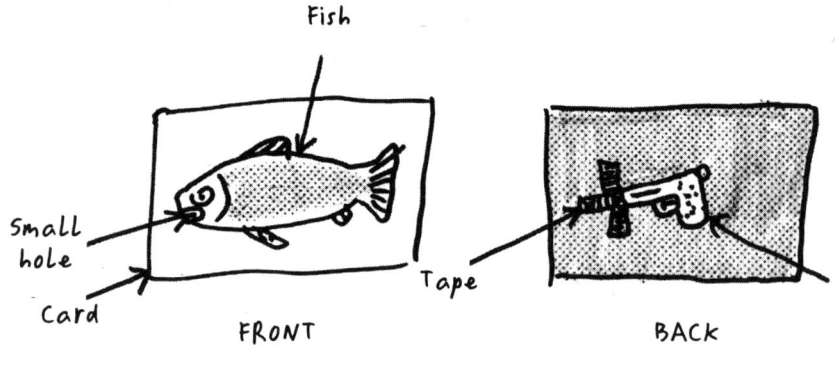

DAY 178

Paint your feet to look like shoes

This is a fun one for a hot summer's day. Get some washable body paint. You can buy it in art shops, toy shops and fancy-dress shops – or, of course, online. Then decide what kind of shoe you'd like to copy – maybe fancy trainers or a more traditional brogue – sit outside, then copy the design onto your feet!

Parade around your garden going, "Hey! Check out my new shoes!"

If you're feeling really fancy and have enough paint left, you could always paint on some socks too!

DAY 179

Discover the lifespan of a boiled sweet

Get a packet of boiled sweets – mints are particularly good for this, especially the ones with the holes.

Suck the first sweet for one minute, take it out and stick it on a piece of card (being a sweet, it should stick itself!). Mark down the number of minutes you've sucked it for underneath.

Suck the second sweet for 2 minutes, the third sweet for 2 x 2 minutes – that's 4 minutes; the fourth for 6 minutes and so on until you've done all of the sweets in the pack. It's probably best not to do this just before dinner time, or you won't be able to manage a pudding. This is the sort of thing that you can come back to over the course of the year.

Behold! You now have a visual guide to the full lifespan of a boiled sweet!

You might like to compare various boiled sweets and how long they last and different ways of sucking them. For instance, does a Polo last longer if you don't move it around much inside your mouth? These are important questions that need urgent answers!!!

Document your results in your silly scrapbook.

The Lifespan of a sweet

1 minute

2 minutes

4 minutes

6 minutes

SILLY FACT NUMBER 20

What do you get if you cross a hedgehog with a tortoise? A tort-hog or a hedge-hoise, but neither are able to live in the wild as hedgehogs, and tortoises won't accept them, so they get very lonely.

The hedge-hoise   The tort-hog

DAY 180

Learn to play the spoons

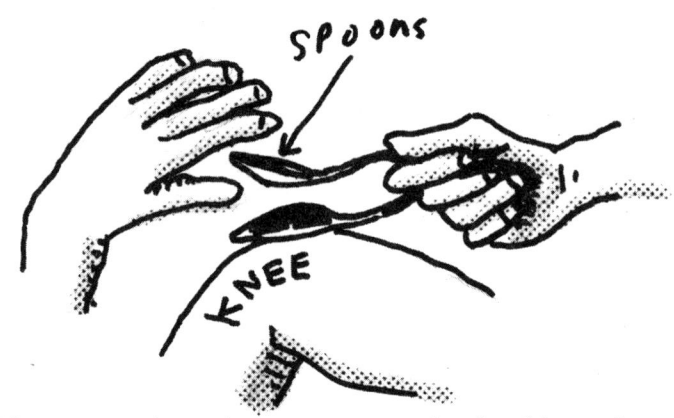

There was a time when everyone used to be able to play the spoons, but sadly, like Debenhams and smallpox, this skill has all but died out. Which is why I'm suggesting we bring it kicking and screaming into the modern era.

Here's how you play the spoons:

* Get two spoons, put them back-to-back in one hand, with your index finger between them.

* Take a seat and then bang the two spoons between your knee and your other hand. Each time the spoons hit either your hand or your knee, they make a clacking noise – this is the signature sound of the spoons!

* You can either sing a song unaccompanied and tap out the rhythm with your spoons or play along to an existing track. Traditionally it was old-fashioned songs like "My Old Man's a Dustman" and "It's a Long Way to Tipperary", but why not try playing the spoons to some chart hits by Miley Cyrus, Dave and Stormzy?

DAY 181

SILLIEST PAGE OF THE BOOK

Paint a picture holding the brush with anything other than your hands.

For instance, try holding the brush or pen in between your toes and doing a portrait of your mum. Or try holding it in your mouth.

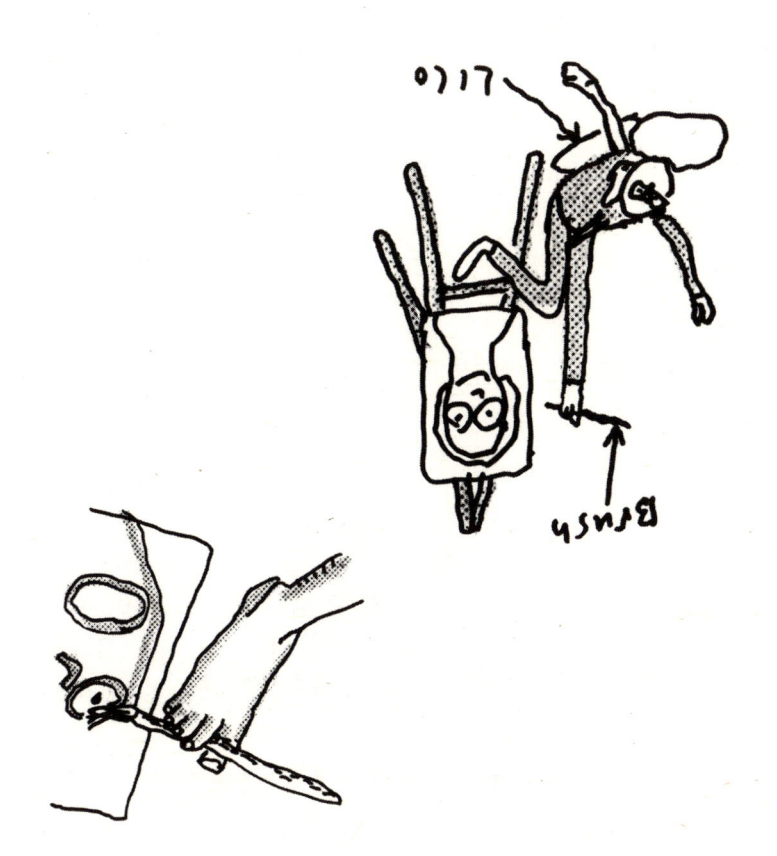

Day 182

Sensible day

Congratulations! You're halfway through, so you've earned yourself a day off. Spend the whole day doing something sensible like tidying your room, cleaning the grout in the shower or cooking a casserole. This will also make you appreciate just how far you've come.

HOORAY!

ADRIAN SENSIBLE
is VERY HAPPY

IF YOU'RE READING THIS SOMEWHERE YOU SHOULDN'T BE (e.g., in a school lesson, whilst eating your dinner or whilst flying a plane) and someone challenges you, turn to **page 158** straight away and say, "Sorry, but I'm reading a really interesting book!"

DAY 183

Motivational day

You're halfway through your silly year and you may be starting to have doubts about why you started it in the first place.* You might be thinking, "It's a lot of work, being silly – is this really the lifestyle for me?" or "I'm tired of being silly every day; I long for the conventional, the straightforward…" or even "Aaagh! I'm going mad!"

Don't Be Alarmed! These feelings are quite normal; everyone goes through this stage – so here are a few motivational quotes to get you over this hump:

* I certainly am!

"The name's silly, very silly."

← A squirrel

D. Trump

W. Shakespeare

"To be silly or not to be silly, that is the question."

"Let's make America silly again."

"$E = M(Silly)^2$"

DAY 184

Supersize a sport

How come you get to play with loads of balls in snooker but only one in most other sports? Try playing football with three balls or tennis with five – it makes it a lot more fun!

DAY 185

Make a butter surprise

Breakfast can be so repetitive, can't it? That's why it's important to keep the surprises coming. Take a regular pat of butter and gently push a small toy such as a Matchbox car, a toy soldier, a tiny doll or plastic dinosaur into it – taking care to smooth it over afterwards so that no one will suspect anything. Then sit back and wait for your pet adult to be surprised when they try to butter their toast!

DAY 186

Random word generator

Next time you're on a car journey, agree with whoever you're travelling with to shout out some random words when you see certain things. Here's what I shout:

"Gas bottles!"
When I see a yellow car

"Angela Lansbury!"
When I see a horse

"Frizzeze!"
When I see a post box

"Lambrusco!"
When I see a caravan

"Bubble trouble!"
Traffic lights

"Man on fire!"
Tractor

"Hedgehog!"
Ambulance

"Jam sandwich!"
Police car

"Flashing penguin!"
Fire engine

"Spratwaffler!"
Bridge

"Huffkin!"
Electric scooter

"Crumpet digger!"
A man with a moustache

"Pifflepot!"
Train

"Grutz!"
Mini roundabout

"Whizzy woo-woo!"
Helicopter

DAY 187

Make an entry system to your room

You're probably like me and wish you had an entry phone system to your house? Well, now you can! All you need is a blister pack like your nan has with her tablets in – but obviously after she's used all the tablets. Throat lozenge packets are good for this too.

Put a sign on your bedroom door that says: PLEASE KNOCK! ENTRY PHONE SYSTEM IN USE. Then, when someone knocks at your door, put the empty blister pack on your forehead and open the door just wide enough to poke your head through, then say, "Press to enter" and encourage the person at the door to press one of the "buttons" on the blister pack.

After they press it, say "Who's calling?" When they say their name, you can decide whether to let them in or not. Once you've decided, you say "Enter!" and open the door, or "I don't know anyone of THAT name. Entry denied!" and close the door.

DAY 188

Create a bunch of real health and safety nightmares

Ever get tired of hearing grown-ups say, "That's a health and safety nightmare!" Me too! Well, why not come up with some dangerous situations that would be actually nightmarish – and draw them. Such as:

* Vacuuming out a rubber dinghy while at sea
* Buying melons on a skateboard
* Walking in shoes decorated with matches on a rug made from the sides of matchboxes
* Juggling chainsaws in a wind tunnel
* Balancing on a pogo stick on a tightrope above a tank full of sharks
* Deep-frying a whole turkey in a lift
* Lighting a fireworks display in a fireworks factory
* Hang-gliding in a china shop

No, no, no!

DAY 189

Learn to speak Marshmallow

Stuff as many marshmallows as you can into your mouth and try to say "fluffy bunny". Keep adding marshmallows until it becomes impossible to say it, then spit them all out! Yuck!

DAY 190

Hide a Rice Krispie

Get a single Rice Krispie and hide it somewhere in your clothes, then get your friends to try and find it. Then it's their turn to hide the Rice Krispie.

Suggested places to hide a Rice Krispie:

* Under your hat
* Behind your ear
* Under your arm
* In the top of your sock
* Between your toes

Hidden Rice Krispie

Any damage to the Rice Krispie results in a forfeit.

DAY 191

Silly five-fits

Come up with some silly forfeits for Hide a Rice Krispie. Things like…

* Stand on one leg for a minute.
* Go up to a friend and ask, "Have the Martians landed yet?"
* Do a chicken impression in a busy shop.
* Swap one of your socks with another player for the rest of the game. You'll have to wear mismatched socks until the game is over.
* Waddle like a penguin for one minute. Bonus points for exaggerated flippers and squawking.
* Bust out your silliest dance moves in a public place. Encourage others to join in for extra silliness.
* Pretend to jump over an invisible rope for thirty seconds. Make it as dramatic and exaggerated as possible.
* Approach a friend or family member with an elaborate and strange "alien" greeting.
* Complete a simple task, like tying your shoelaces or drinking from a cup, while blindfolded.

DAY 192

Make a portable shadow

On a sunny day, step outside and position yourself so that you've got a nice shadow. Put down a large piece of card, or unroll a length of leftover wallpaper, and get someone to trace round your shadow with a pencil.

Cut out your shadow then fill it in with grey paint. Once it's dry, save it for an overcast day when there's no sun. Then stand at the bus stop or in the playground or in your garden and unroll the shadow – doesn't it just make you feel all summery?

DAY 193

Try on multiple glasses

See how many pairs of glasses you can wear in one go.

DAY 194

Espresso bongo

Get an old pair of shoes and attach a whole load of those coffee capsules that are all the rage to the soles of them. Hey, presto – you've got the world's first pair of coffee-capsule-soled shoes!

Walk around outside in them for a bit. Not indoors, as you might get coffee everywhere. If anyone asks you what kind of shoes you're wearing, sing this song:

> *I like coffee!*
> *I like tea!*
> *I like coffee capsules on my feet!*
> *Coffee capsules*
> *On my feet.*
> *I really, really, really, really*
> *Think they're neat!*

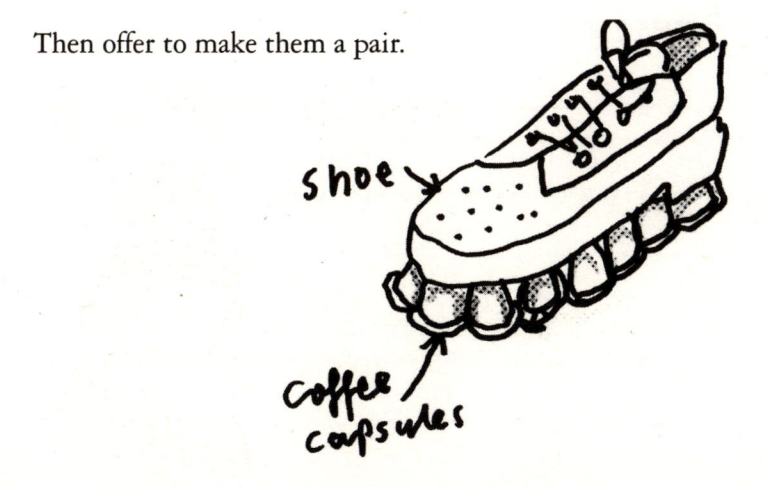

Then offer to make them a pair.

Make some silly stickers

Get some plain stickers like your mum might use to return parcels full of clothes that she didn't like, or that your dad puts on parcels full of light bulbs that have the wrong fitting.* Take these plain stickers and write silly but important messages on them. Things like ...

- ➡ THIS WAY FOR THE FREE POTATOES
- WATCH OUT FOR THE TEDDY BEARS!
- THE TEDDY BEARS ARE COMING!
- STOP THE ATOMIC SCOOTERS!
- SAY **NO** TO THE SOLAR-POWERED TOLL BRIDGE!
- SUPPORT ISI (Important Sticker Information)
- I'D RATHER BE **FRYING EGGS!**
- FEATHERS SHOULD STAY ON BIRDS!
- DOGS ARE HUMAN TOO!
- MY OTHER GOLDFISH ISN'T THAT STICKY!

You know, IMPORTANT stuff! Then take your stickers and stick them up in unlikely places such as on your grandad's shed.

* Hands up, this happened to me. I needed light bulbs with a bayonet fitting but accidentally ordered screw-ins!

DAY 196

Sandal handle

Attach a sandal to your bedroom door handle.

DAY 197

Have a pillow fight

POW!

Everyone should have at least one pillow fight a year and today's the day for yours! If your mum or dad complains, just explain that you're "plumping up the pillows".

If any feathers spill out of the pillows, check to see if any of them are your pet feather from earlier in the year. If you see my feather – Frankie Frankenfeather – please tell him "hi!".

SILLY PEOPLE FROM HISTORY NUMBER 412: YVES KLEIN

Yves Klein (1928–1962) was a painter who painted pictures using other people's bodies as his paintbrushes. I bet bathtime was messy!

YVES KLEIN

DAY 198

Make some pop-heads

Get some of those toy plastic soldiers – you know, the green ones which are all stuck in various aggressive poses like sniper! Or attack! Or skipping!*

Take one of the soldiers, then buy or make some popcorn. Push the largest piece of popcorn you can find onto the soldier's head so it covers it completely. You might need to make a bit of a hole with a cocktail stick for the head first.

It doesn't matter if some of the pieces of popcorn break off – in fact, it's quite good because you can eat them. If anyone asks what happened to your soldier, tell them, "His head exploded."

SILLY FACT NUMBER 21
Famous for their love of shiny objects, like rings and jewels, magpies these days are increasingly going contactless.

* OK, not skipping – I just put that in to check that you were still paying attention…

DAY 199

Welcome to Team Silly

Today you're going to put together the silliest team in the whole world!

Just as on **Day 55**, when we made a silly magazine using collage, today we're going to use those same skills to make a really, really, really, really silly team photo.

The easiest way to do this is to take an existing team photo – from a newspaper, magazine or printed from the internet – and simply stick new heads on them. It can be a football team, a rugby team, a darts team, a netball team – whatever you like. You might have Scooby-Doo in defence, Fiona Bruce in midfield, Sonic the Hedgehog in attack, and a Tyrannosaurus rex in goal.

You can put whoever you want from all of history in your team! Don't forget to put yourself in the picture – after all, you are the captain!

DAY 200

Design a silly mascot

Design a mascot for your silly team. The famous artist David Shrigley designed this mascot called Kingsley for his favourite football team, Partick Thistle.

Kingsley – the mascot of Partick Thistle Football Club

"H" – the mascot of Team Harry

"S" – the mascot of Team Stouffer

Maybe you can do better?

DAY 201

Make your silly mascot live!

Attempt to make the mascot you designed yesterday. If you can't make a full-size costume, make it to fit one of your Barbies, Action Men or teddies. It can be made from fabric, cardboard or paper.

DAY 202

Sleeping partner

Leave your silly mascot in your friend's bed without telling them, as a surprise.

DAY 203 — **SILLY SCRIBBLES NUMBER 4**

Draw a mattress flying a plane. Where's the plane going? Probably to an important business meeting or maybe to see all its friends at the airport! Partaaaay! That's what I call an air mattress!

SILLY FACT NUMBER 23

New "eco" batteries are being developed that contain an ant powering a tiny treadmill. At one end of the battery, there is a sugar lump, which the ant uses as fuel; at the other end is a chill-out zone for the ant, so it has something to look forward to when it's not working.

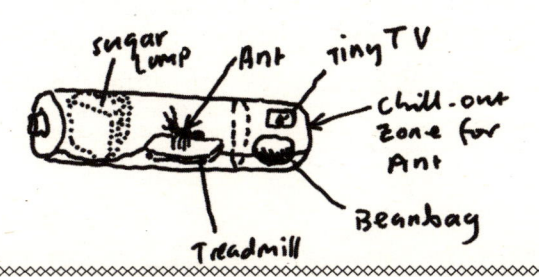

DAY 204

Balloon folding

Ask someone if they'd like to see a demonstration of the ancient art of balloon folding. Then get any old balloon, a round one, a straight one – it really doesn't matter.

No need to blow it up – just carefully fold the deflated balloon in half and say, "There, the ancient art of balloon folding!"

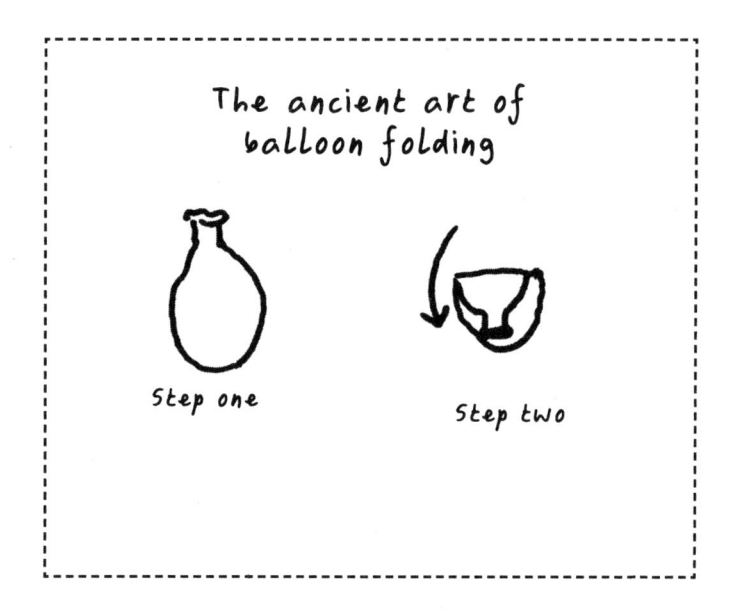

If you're taking a balloon on holiday, it's good to know how to fold it!

The ancient art of balloon folding

Step one   Step two

DAY 205

Proper balloon folding

OK, so you need some proper balloon-folding balloons for this – the long thin ones. You can get them online and they're quite cheap. If you want a discount, just quote this code: `TH1515N0TR3411YAC0D3`.*

Obviously, there are all the shapes that every balloon folder makes – the swan, the sausage dog ... yawn ... boring!

I'd like you to come up with your own designs, please. Like "The Scribble", "The Snake" and "The My Dad's Signature When He Asks for the Bill in a Restaurant".

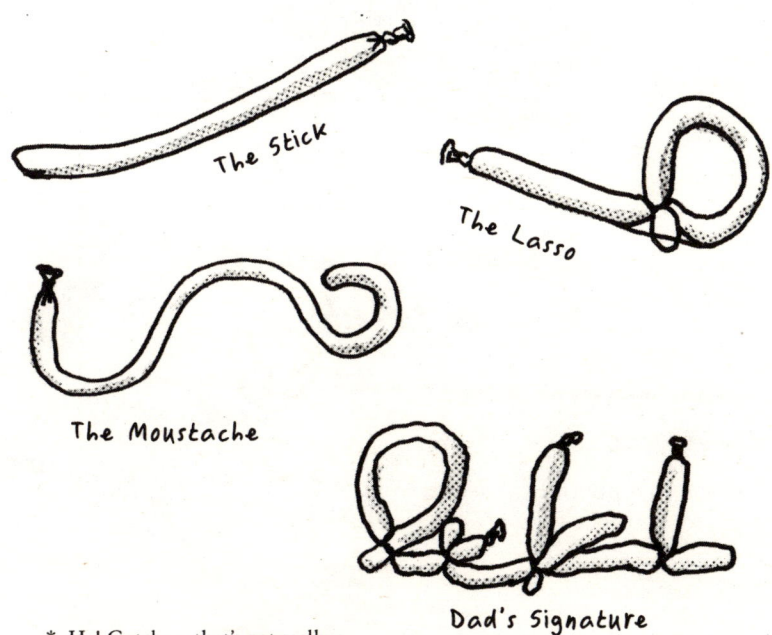

The Stick

The Lasso

The Moustache

Dad's Signature

* Ha! Gotcha – that's not really a discount code. In fact, if you look at it again, it says "THIS IS NOT REALLY A CODE".

DAY 206

Become part of the landscape

Get a piece of fake grass – you know, the stuff you can get in rolls that's a bit like grassy carpet. You'll need about a metre and a half depending on how tall you are. Cut eye holes and lie under it in the garden and see how long it takes for someone to tread on you.

DANGER! Don't do this when someone's cutting the grass. Oh, and keep away from dogs!

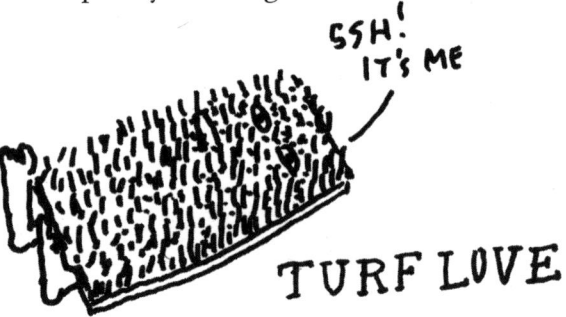

SSH! IT'S ME

TURF LOVE

Teach a wave a trick

DAY 207

Next time you go to the beach, train a wave to jump through a hoop. Practise in the bath.

JUMP!

A WAVE

DAY 208

Size up your life

Go to the post office with random items and, using the Royal Mail Size Guide, see if they count as a letter, a large letter or a small package.

Suggested items for sizing:

- A slice of bread
- A flip-flop
- A wooden spoon
- A lilo

The Royal Mail Sizing Guide

DAY 209

Start a Museum of Silly

Wouldn't it be great to have a whole load of silly things in one place? Of course it would! Which is why I'm suggesting you put together your very own Silly Museum.

Take items that would normally be heading for the bin, glue them to pieces of card and label them up with the details on little bits of paper like you see in a serious museum.

Things like ...

- * Rishi Sunak's flip-flop (it's just any old flip-flop really, but no one else knows that)
- * The toenail clippings of Adele
- * The fluff from Queen Camilla's belly button*

---

* I have actually got some of this – don't ask how. If you want any, just send a stamped addressed envelope and details of the amount you need.

Or it could be a museum dedicated to one silly thing, like bottle tops, hubcaps or sticks that look like famous entertainers (I've got a stick that's the spitting image of Rylan).

If you think I'm going mad, HERE'S A LIST OF RANDOM MUSEUMS THAT ACTUALLY EXIST:

- Beijing Tap Water Museum
- The Dog Collar Museum, Leeds Castle, Kent
- The British Lawnmower Museum, Merseyside
- The Instant Noodle Museum, Japan

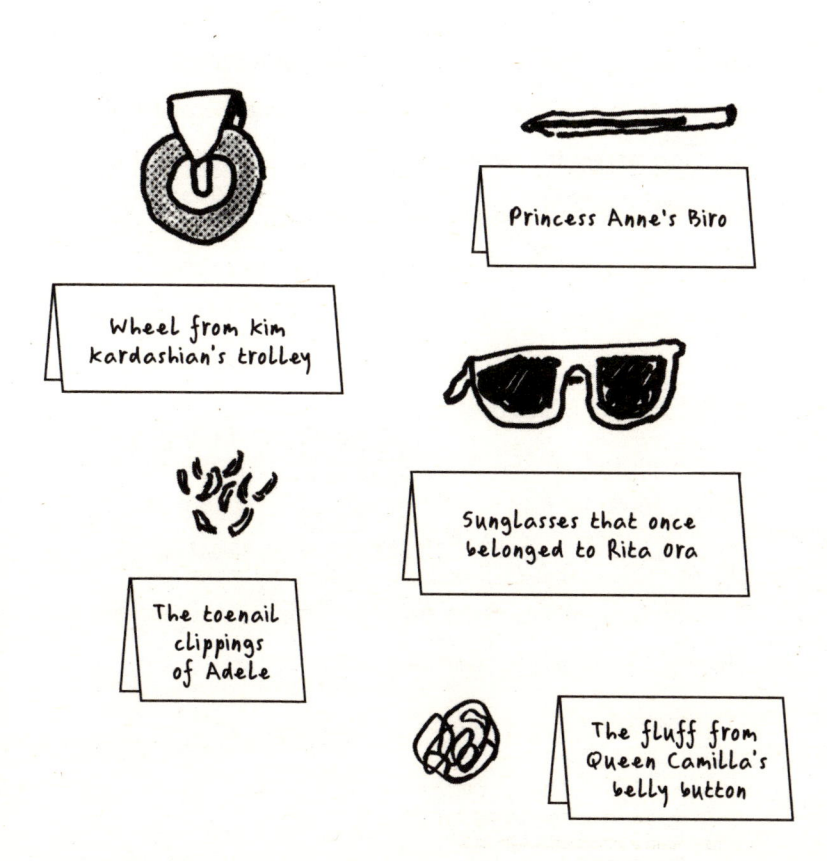

Wheel from Kim Kardashian's trolley

Princess Anne's Biro

The toenail clippings of Adele

Sunglasses that once belonged to Rita Ora

The fluff from Queen Camilla's belly button

DAY 210

Don't forget the gift shop!

As a politician once said, "Never miss a chance to make some hard cash from a silly idea." So don't forget the gift shop. It's in the gift shop that you can sell some of the silly souvenirs you've made so far – like your silly potatoes, silly stickers or even void-fill sculptures (see **Day 245**).

Make sure you put lots of signs up around the gift shop area telling people how to behave – stuff like: "YOU DON'T HAVE TO BE SILLY TO WORK HERE, BUT IT HELPS!", "SMILE, OR BETTER STILL, START TAP-DANCING – THIS SHOP IS ON CCTV!" and "IF YOU BREAK ANYTHING – I'LL TELL YOUR MUM!"

Use any money you make from the shop for a donation to charity – or just buy yourself some sweets.

DAY 211

Rescue some baked beans

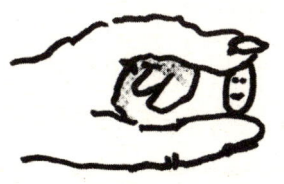

Today you're going to save some baked beans from drowning by rescuing them from their sauce. Empty a small tin of beans into a bowl and, using your fingers or a fork, fish out the baked beans.

Dry them off with a tiny towel. As you do this, say something like "Everything's OK, you're safe now!" just to reassure the beans that their nightmare is over.

Beans relaxing on towels

Congratulations, you're a hero! Tell them to be more careful in future when playing around sauce.

DAY 212

Make a message tube

Before telephones were invented, people would communicate with each other via a system of tubes... I think! Anyway, that's what we're going to try to do today.

I hope you've still got your biscuit delivery tube? (**Day 154 – REMEMBER?**) Get another empty cardboard toilet roll tube and cut a slit in it lengthways.

Overlap the edges to reduce the diameter of the tube by about half and tape it up. You've now got a cardboard tube about half as wide as the biscuit-delivery flume – yes? Block up one end by taping something heavy to it – something like a pebble or a couple of pound coins or even a lead fishing weight if you've got one. Attach the open end to a piece of string or fishing line that's at least as long as your flume.

Stick the flume down the stairs and get the person you want to receive the message to stand at the other end.

Write your message on a small piece of paper, roll it up, stuff it into the tube and lower it down the flume to the person waiting at the other end.

The second person replies to the message then gives a tug on the piece of string. This acts as a signal for you to pull the message back up the flume.

The other thing you can do is get them to put their end of the tube to their ear while you speak into your end – but the problem with that is you'll have no record of what was said.

DAY 213

Hold the front page!

Design the front page of a newspaper that's reporting the great baked bean rescue of **Day 211**. What would the headline be? BEAN THERE, DONE THAT! YOU'VE BEAN SAVED! or A NUMBER OF BEANS RESCUED FROM SOME SAUCE!

Draw a picture of some part of the rescue, then write your report, including interviews with the survivor beans and of course with you, the hero of the day.

DAY 214

Partay like it's 2034

I love a party as much as anyone, but I'm kind of a little bit bored of playing the same games over and over again. That's why I've come up with a new one – instead of Pin the Tail on the Donkey, how about Pin the Ears on the Celebrity?

Simply take a photo of a celebrity like Beyoncé, Gareth Southgate or Gemma Collins. If you know one or live next door to one that's easy, but if not, just cut one out of

BEYONCÉ KNOWLES

NICK KNOWLES

Not to be confused with...

a magazine or print one off the internet. Now draw a pair of big ears on a piece of paper and cut them out. Put some Blu Tack on the back of each one, and you're ready to go.

Stick the picture of the celeb on the wall and take it in turns to wear a blindfold, be spun round and try to place the ears either side of their head. If you've got a camera, it's worth filming this, as people love to see themselves stumbling around getting it wrong. The person who pins the ears closest to the celeb's own ears wins.

It doesn't have to be a celebrity — or, in fact, ears. It could be Pin the Nose on Your Mum or Pin the Tongue on your Nan. Either way, it's a very, very silly game.

Whosoever this ear fits, I shall marry!

DAY 215

Learn some great jokes

Learn ten jokes and get a couple of friends to agree to learn ten jokes each too so you can hold a comedy night.

The best place to find good jokes is in the *Harry Hill's Whopping Great Joke Book*, which is available in all good bookshops – and some bad ones too! Or better still, write your own jokes.

DAY 216

Mix up your fruit

Put a lemon in an apple tree and watch how people react to it. If you haven't got an apple tree – put a lemon in any old tree or hang it off a rose bush.

DAY 217

Learn some heckle put-downs

If you're planning a comedy night (see **Day 218**), you'll need to learn a few heckle put-downs, just in case. A heckle is where a member of the audience shouts something out to put the comedian off. Here are some of my favourites:

"You've got a brain, but it hasn't reached your head!"

"Would you mind closing the door – from the OUTSIDE!"

"I can make funnier faces than you – even though you've got a head start on me!"

"You may think you're the big cheese around here – but you just smell like it!"

"That's a nice suit you're wearing, but the horse wants it back!"

"Your haircut must cost you four pounds – a pound for each corner!"

"I'd like to help you out – which way did you come in?"

Is that a moustache, or have your EYEBROWS come down for a drink?

DAY 218

Hold a comedy night

Er... testing...

Once you've learnt the jokes and a couple of heckle put-downs, hold a comedy night. It doesn't have to be anywhere fancy – it could just be in your front room in front of your family and friends or, if you're feeling really confident, you could ask your teacher whether you could hold it at school.

Decide which one of you wants to be the compere, or the MC of the comedy night – that person goes on first, tells a few jokes and then introduces the other acts. Ideally the gig would go ...

- Compere warms up audience and introduces the first act
- First act (5 minutes)
- Compere thanks the first act and introduces the second act
- Second act (10 minutes)
- Compere thanks the second act and introduces a short interval
- Interval
- Compere welcomes back the audience and introduces the third act
- Third act (10 minutes – or maybe a bit longer)
- Compere thanks the third act, thanks the audience for coming and tells them about the next comedy night.

If you're feeling really confident about your jokes, you could try to sell tickets for the event. You should then use this money to invest in better lighting and possibly a state-of-the-art sound system. Or just split it between your friends and buy some sweets. Or, if you're feeling really nice, donate it to charity.

SILLY FACT NUMBER 12

Blu Tack is actually made from that lump of grey stuff on a pigeon's beak. It takes 48 pigeons to make one packet of Blu Tack.

DAY 219

Make a sock puppet

Get an old white sock and draw a face on it with a pen. Give it a name. Suggested names for a sock puppet:

* Brian
* Ian Crackerjack
* Mo Housebrick
* Annastasia Gumdrop
* Vaclav Stickelback
* Steve Gum
* Brenda Creosote
* Jean-Claude Van Hammock

Although I call my sock puppet "Stinky" for reasons I can't go into.

Wear the sock puppet wherever you go, and when someone says something, get the puppet to answer for you. See how long you can go without speaking as yourself.

I once went six months as Stinky the Sock, so good luck beating that!

DAY 220

Put your sock to work

The next time you're going on a long car journey, take your sock puppet with you. When you pull up next to another car at the traffic lights, sink down below the level of the window and pop the sock puppet up as if he's the passenger. Unfortunately, you won't be able to see their reactions – but you can be sure they'll be surprised!

DAY 221

Feed your brother with a long spoon

Attach a spoon to a broom handle with tape or some string and attempt to feed a friend or your brother some yoghurt. Do this outside, or your mum and dad will kill you.

Other foods you can try are jelly, rice pudding, blancmange and soup.

DAY 222

DIY tattoos

Tattoos are all the rage, aren't they? You've probably got an older sister who came back from her holiday in Ibiza plastered with ink. In fact, my nan had a map of the UK tattooed all over her body. You might think that's a strange idea – but say what you like about my nan, you always knew where you were with her.

The problem with tattoos is it all looks a bit painful, doesn't it? That's why I've come up with the next best thing…

Get a friend to draw round you on a large piece of paper or card, then cut it out. For decency's sake put an actual pair of pants on the paper version of you, or, if they won't fit, draw or paint them on. Then cover the rest of the body in a selection of tattoos.

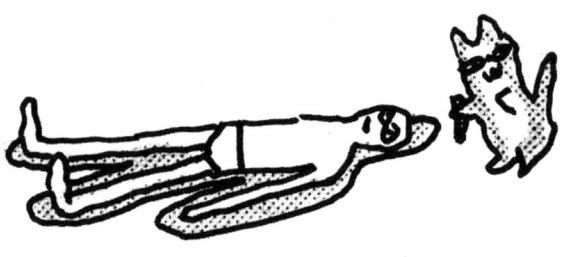

See if you can cover pretty much the whole body with them. If you can't get a giant piece of paper, then just draw an outline of yourself on a piece of A4 paper. It doesn't have to be you – it could be your mum or your head teacher.

Suggested tattoos:

* Giant mermaid
* Heart with arrow through it and two pairs of initials
* Skull with snake coming out of the eye socket
* Ford Fiesta on fire
* Pork chop
* Skipping lamb
* Pair of pants on a washing line
* Smiley potato
* Slogans like: "My other tattoo is actually a birthmark" or "This tattoo once belonged to David Beckham!"

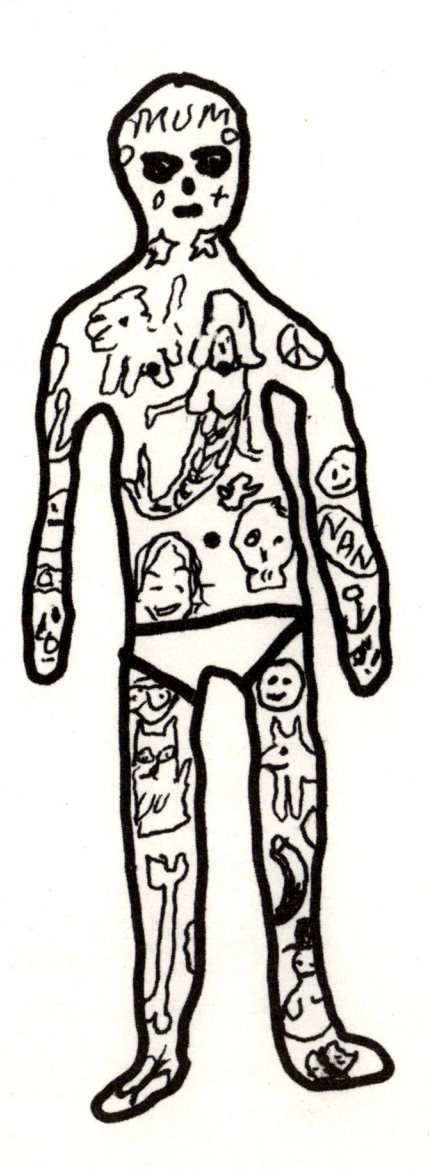

DAY 223

Make a pop-star trap

We all love pop stars. I'm fond of Gary Barlow, the lead singer and creative force behind singing group Take It from That — but wouldn't it be nice to keep your fave star to yourself? Here's how to make a pop-star trap!

I'm Gary Barlow! I LOVE Eccles cakes!

Hi, Gary!

Get a wheelie bin, turn it on its side, and place something inside that will attract a pop star, like an Eccles cake, a roast chicken or a photo of the Bee Gees.

Prop the lid of the wheelie bin open with a stick and wait.

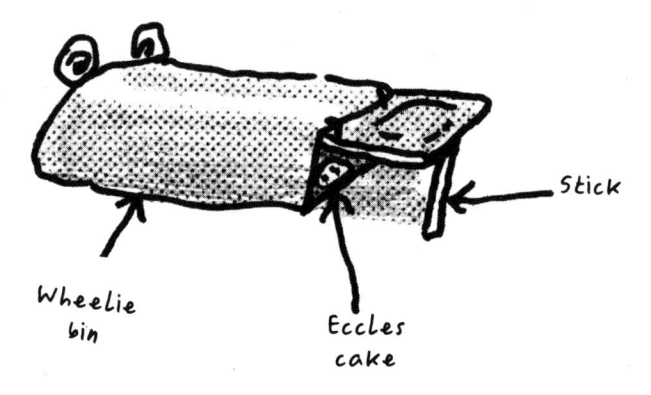

Wheelie bin — Eccles cake — Stick

What should happen is that a pop star will eventually wander by, see the reward and crawl inside the wheelie bin to retrieve it. As they do so, their back leg will kick away the stick and the wheelie bin lid will close behind them, trapping them inside.

Congratulations, you just caught yourself an A-lister! Make sure you don't leave them in the bin for too long, or they will become agitated.

The great news is that, when you release your pop star, they'll be so grateful they'll keep in touch with offers of free tickets to their shows.

It doesn't have to be a pop-star trap – it could be anyone you're keen to meet. Here's a list of suggested people and what to use as bait:

* **Ronan Keating** – salad
* **Fiona Bruce** – antique ceramic cat
* **Olly Murs** – KitKat Chunky
* **Stephen Mulhern** – duck in hoisin sauce wrap
* **Taylor Swift** – Network SouthEast railcard

DAYS 224 AND 225

Set up a fly rescue centre

Picture of a fly

Fly chillin' on a towel

Bowl of sugar

Spare towels

How come everyone's hating on flies the whole time? Truth is, we need them now more than ever – so let's look after them.

First, take a cardboard box – a shoe box is a good size – and write "Fly Rescue Centre" on the outside of it in big letters so that all the flies can see it.

On the base of the inside of the cardboard box, draw boxes a couple of centimetres in size – these are the individual areas for the flies to relax. Put a tiny square of kitchen roll inside the boxes for the flies to lie on. You might like to put up some pictures of flies to make them feel at home and put a bowl of sugar for the flies in the middle of the box with a message: "Flies, help yourselves!"

Once word gets out about the fly rescue centre, you'll find that flies will come and book in for a couple of days to chill out and generally recharge their batteries.

You'll need rules, though! You don't want any other insects using your facilities – and especially not spiders! So you need to put a list of rules on a sticker outside your fly rescue centre. You'll probably come up with some good rules of your own, but here are some of mine:

FRC RULES
1. No spiders
2. No mammals
3. No amphibians
4. No marsupials (except in exceptional circumstances)
5. No time wasters
6. No unaccompanied WASPS.

SILLY PEOPLE FROM HISTORY NUMBER 6: FRANCIS HENRY EGERTON

Egerton (1756–1829), the 8th Earl of Bridgewater, held dinner parties for dogs. The dogs were asked to dress in the fanciest fashions of the day, finished off with a nice pair of shoes.

Caesar salad, yum!

DAY 226

Create a savoury monster

Honey Monster, Cookie Monster ... how come the sweet items get a monster but the savoury ones never do? Well, they do now! Get ready to meet the Plain Naan Monster!

You'll need:

* A plain naan
* A large rubber band, like the ones that the postman leaves behind on your front step

1. Take the naan and attach it to your face with the rubber band. Mark on it where your eyes and mouth are with a pen. Take the naan off your face and tear out holes for the eyes and mouth.

2. Now put it back on your face with the rubber band and you're pretty much ready to go. You might like to think about what Plain Naan Monster wears (I suggest a T-shirt with "PLAIN NAAN MONSTER" written on in marker pen, a pair of shorts and plimsolls or trainers – possibly with pitta breads stuck over them).

3. Then, when you're ready, hide behind a door or behind the sofa and rear up, making a weird monster noise.

4. Suggested noise:

Naaaaaaaaaaaaaan!

Then run out of the room before anyone gets a chance to work out it's you.

DAY 227

Repurpose your soft toys

If you've had enough of a soft toy – you know, a teddy that's just not doing it for you any more – then why not convert it into a puppet and give it a whole new lease of life?

Simply take your tired old teddy or your boring Barney the Dinosaur, make a hole in the back of it big enough for your hand, pull all the stuffing out of it and, before you know it, you've got a puppet that's headlining at your second comedy night!

An important thing to consider if your puppet is going to go on to have a long and successful career in show business – like Basil Brush or Kermit the Frog – is what their personality is. Here are a few options:

* Rude puppet
* Ill puppet
* Puppet that tells jokes
* Puppet that knows a lot about antiques

At this point I'm going to hand you over to my pet cat, Stouffer, who is a puppet expert and who also happens to know a lot of puppets.

> Hello, everyone! It's me, Stouffer! Harry's blue cat! I hope you're enjoying his book – I'm still on Day 4! Now it's important for any puppet to have some good jokes.

Here are some jokes Harry told me!

Stouffer jokes

STOUFFER:	Harry?
HARRY:	Yes, Stouffer?
STOUFFER:	I was walking along eating a bag of chocolates when some tiny people started taking the mickey out of me!
HARRY:	Small teasers?
STOUFFER:	No, M&Ms!
HARRY:	That's a terrible joke, Stouffer!
STOUFFER:	Here's one you might like! Why did the flea stick out its tiny thumbs?
HARRY:	I don't know, why did the flea stick out its tiny thumbs?
STOUFFER:	Because he was ITCHIN' a ride!
HARRY:	Oh dear!
STOUFFER:	Why did the hip-hop magician say he hated the amusements at Brighton?
HARRY:	Make this the last one please, Stouffer.
STOUFFER:	OK. He wanted to diss-a-pier. Ha!

That's enough now, Stouffer.

DAY 228

Plan a trip to a desert island

Ever wondered what you'd do if you got stranded on a desert island? No? Well, you should do because it might happen.

MMM, I fancy some CHIPS!

Draw out a plan of the camp you would build, taking into consideration where you'd sleep, where you'd wash, what you'd use for a kitchen and where you'd go to the toilet. Make a list of some of the stuff you'd want to take with you. Here's mine:

Stuff I'd take to a desert island

- MY MUM
- MY WELLIES
- MATCHES
- CANDLES
- LAMB CHOP
- CHIPS
- WATER
- FIZZY DRINKS
- Air Freshener
- REBEKAH VARDY
- SWEETS

DAY 229

Go land swimming

Isn't it annoying when you'd like to go swimming but are nowhere near an open expanse of water? Why not do what I do and go "land swimming". The good news is you don't need a towel and you don't need to get changed – and you don't need to worry about your breathing. The only slight downside is that the only stroke you can do is front crawl.

The best places for land swimming are on a polished wood or lino floor or on carpet, but you can also do it on grass – but maybe check it for any sharp stones or … er … dog muck.

It might be better, if you're swimming outside, to lie on a skateboard – just so your clothes don't get too dirty.

Why not organize a land swimming gala! But please, no diving!

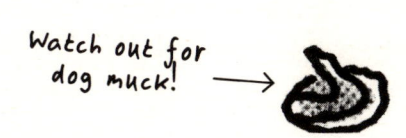

Watch out for dog muck!

DAY 230

Organize a bread versus veg fight

Organize a fight between a cucumber and a bread roll. The winner fights a courgette.

vs.

DAY 231

How to remember to be silly

Occasionally you may find yourself forgetting to be silly and having lapses into seriousness. Here's how to remember to be silly…

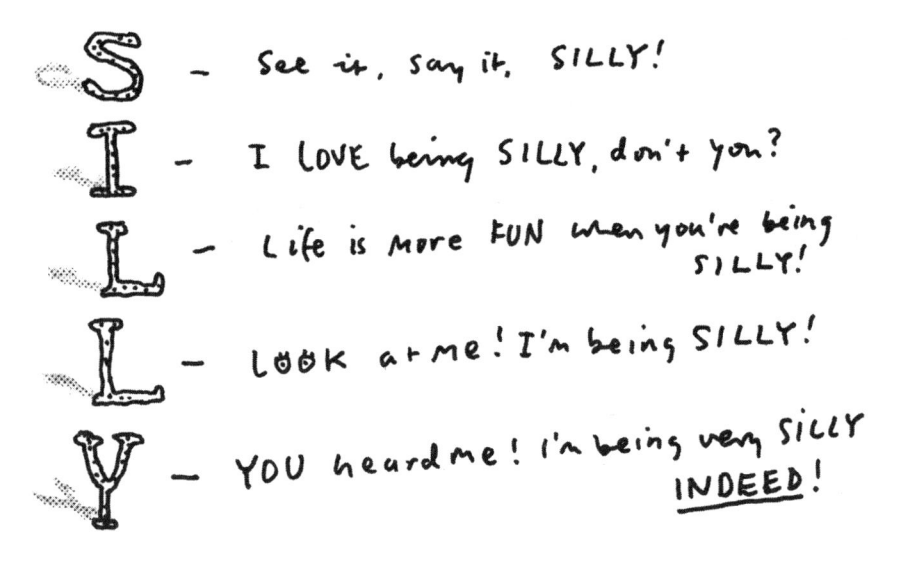

S — See it, say it, SILLY!

I — I LOVE being SILLY, don't you?

L — Life is more FUN when you're being SILLY!

L — LOOK at me! I'm being SILLY!

Y — YOU heard me! I'm being very SILLY INDEED!

DAY 232

Meet the Crisp Family

Open a bag of crisps and place them one by one onto a piece of paper.

Draw round each one, then give them all names (Brian is a nice name). You might like to place them in family groups, so maybe you'd have the Edwards family of crisps, with Mum and Dad Edwards and their two sons – Cyril and Eddie – and three daughters – Kitty, Winifred and Frederica. Then you'd have the Maris-Piper family, the Jersey Royals and so on.

Eat the crisps, then learn the names of the crisps from their outlines. Get a friend to test you on the names. It also works with Quavers but is much harder as they all look so similar.

THE CRISP FAMILY

Hi, I'm Brian Edwards and here is my wife, Brenda...

Hello!

My sons Cyril

Hi

... Eddie

Hi there!

And three daughters ...

Hello! Hello! Hello!

Kitty, Winifred and Frederica.

DAY 233

Set up a soft toy shooting range

You're probably like me and, although you have one or two favourite soft toys (for me, it's Tiggy the knitted tiger), you're probably starting to think, "Hey! I'm nine! Stop buying me soft toys, Auntie, and instead give me electronic goods – or, better still, hard cash so I can go and buy my own electronic goods!"

I'll say it again, if you're reading this and thinking, "Wait a minute! I love all my soft toys! I just can't get enough of them! Every morning, I wake up and long for more soft toys!", I'm giving you permission to skip this challenge.

If you haven't got any spare soft toys, don't even think about borrowing your little sister's, because you'll get into trouble – and so will I (and I've been in enough trouble lately what with throwing toilet roll tubes down the stairs and getting a chewing-gum ghost all over my mum's new cushions). The truth is, you can get VERY cheap soft toys from charity shops.

> **You'll need:**
> * At least one soft toy
> * Some string or wool
> * A tree or lamppost
> * A pea-shooter (see **Day 84**)
> * Some mushed-up paper rolled into peas

Hey! Why can't I be turned into a puppet like the hamster?!

What to do:

Tie your soft toy to the tree so it can't escape – I know this is unlikely, but you can't be too careful ... you never know whether another bunch of soft toys might try to rescue it. Then pick up your pea-shooter and, from a suitable distance – let's say eight paces from the tree? – on the command of "One ... two ... three ... FIRE!" you let rip!

Remember to untie the soft toy at the end and give him a bath or a decent send-off.

DAY 234

Build a cheese igloo

Get the largest round cracker you can find – Bath Olivers are good for this – then ask a pet adult to help you cut up a block of nice strong Cheddar cheese into cubes (these will become your building blocks). Stack the cubes in ever-decreasing circles around the edge of the cracker to create your igloo. You might need to use some cheese spread or butter as cement, particularly for the top.

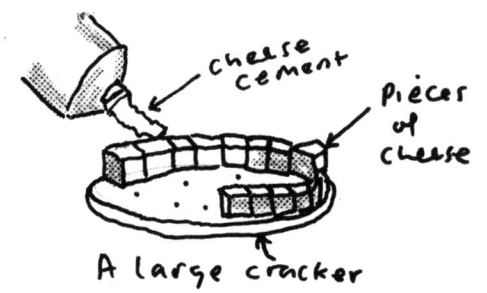

Once you've built your igloo, build some other cheese houses such as an office block or the Southbank Centre – cheese lends itself particularly well to Brutalist architecture! These cheese buildings are very tasty with a pickled onion.

DAY 235

Communicate only with a musical instrument for a day

Grab your carrot whistle,* your nose flute or a tambourine, electronic keyboard, toy xylophone or a triangle – in fact, any musical instrument you can get your hands on, and when someone asks you a question, answer only using the musical instrument. For example:

> MUM: Have you got any homework?
>
> ME (on the trombone):
>   Root-tee-toot-tee-toot-tee-toot!
>
> MUM: Maths and history?
>
> ME: Toot!

Let me know how you get on!

* See Day 94: Make a root toot.

DAY 236

Pick up a bargain

At the supermarket checkout, take the "NEXT CUSTOMER" sign and when the person on the till asks you what you're buying, point to it and say, "That, please."

DAY 237

SILLY SCRIBBLES NUMBER 6

So, you built some accommodation out of cheese. Now I want you to imagine you're a mouse discovering a house made from cheese! Draw the mouse's face. Here's what I think it would look like…

I DON'T BELIEVE IT! A CHEESE IGLOO!

DAY 238

Create a voice from nowhere

This one is really good fun but involves a couple of things you might not have – i.e., a smart speaker and a smartphone. If you can get your hands on these, then read on, because this one is a lot of fun.

Basically, you're going to record some stuff on the phone and play it back through the smart speaker, but here's the silly bit: you're going to hide the smart speaker in a silly place so the person hearing the recording will think it's coming from there.

It's probably best if I just give you a few examples:

* Put the smart speaker under your parents' bed and play back ghostly noises at night.
* Put it down the back of the sofa and play your recording – "I'm a mouse and I'm stuck inside the sofa!" while they're watching *Coronation Street*.

* Hide it in a bush and talk to a passerby as if you are the bush. "Hello! I'm a bush! Nice day, isn't it?" and "Would you mind getting a watering can? I'm very thirsty!"

HELLO! I'M A BUSH!

AAGH!

A. SERIOUS

* Stick it in the dog's bed and record stuff like it's the dog talking: "Any chance of a biscuit?" or "Excuse me, but when are you taking me out for a walk?" You'll need to practise your dog voice, though!

* Hide the smart speaker in the bathroom. The next time someone goes to use the toilet, try playing the national anthem so they have to stand up!

GOD SAVE THE KING!

DAYS 239 AND 240

Train a cucumber to do a back flip

This is a great trick for family gatherings or parties – or for amazing your friends.

> **You'll need:**
>
> * Scissors
> * A cardboard box
> * Parcel tape
> * Some newspaper, shredded into 2 cm strips
> * An old pair of gloves
> * Double-sided sticky tape
> * A cucumber

Cut the cardboard box down so it's more like a tray (approximately 20 cm high). You may need to reinforce any seams with parcel tape.

Cut a hole in one of the long sides on either the left if you're left-handed, or the right if you mainly use your right hand. Stuff the glove with the shredded newspaper so it looks more like a hand.

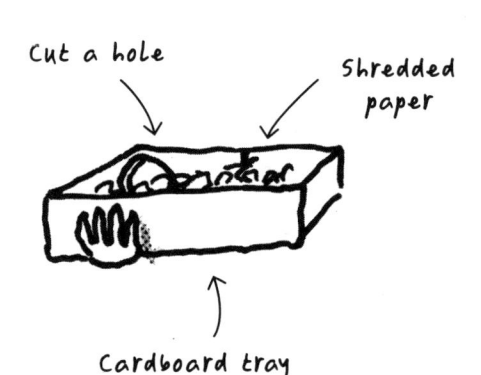

Cut a hole → *Shredded paper* ↙
↑ *Cardboard tray*

Stuff a rubber glove with paper

Attach the hand to the outside of the box opposite the hole so it looks like it's holding the box (you might need to use double-sided sticky tape to really hold it in place). Get your pet adult to help you with this step – but make sure they promise not to reveal how the trick is done.

Half fill the cardboard tray with the rest of the shredded newspaper, then place the hand holding the cucumber through the hole, taking care to hide it under the shredded paper. Put the other glove on your other hand, which should now be holding the tray. It should look from the front as if you're holding the tray with two hands, and your audience shouldn't be able to see INTO or UNDER the box. Practise this in front of the mirror so that you've got the angle right.

Go up to a friend or family member and explain that you've been training a cucumber to do back flips – the more elaborate the story, the funnier the surprise. Something like…

"Many years ago, I found myself in ASDA, and as I approached the salad items, I noticed that one of the cucumbers was twitching in the chiller cabinet. I quickly put it in my basket and took it home. It was the best £1.00 I've ever spent, for I discovered that it was a genetically modified cucumber that could be trained to perform gymnastics. I have spent the last three weeks training it to perform a back flip for you today!"

Then you command the cucumber to jump by saying something like "One ... two ... three ... hup!" and, with your hidden hand (the one holding the cucumber) you toss the cucumber into the air. No one will be expecting it to jump at all!

DAY 241 *Put a moustache on a baby*

In fact, don't do this one – just draw a moustache on a photo of a baby instead, or stick the moustache on your nan when she's asleep.

DAY 242 *Contact all the rabbits!*

You'll need a box of matches with just one match in it for this. You go up to someone and say, "How do you get hold of all the rabbits in Kent?"*

Then you take a match out of the matchbox and stick it in the top of the box so it's sticking up like an aerial and speak into the matchbox like it's an old-fashioned walkie-talkie: "Calling all rabbits! Calling all rabbits!"

* It doesn't have to be Kent; it's just that I happen to be in Kent...

DAY 243
Learn a song backwards

Try learning a song backwards well. The words are sung backwards, but the tune is forwards. Here's a simple one to start:

How Much Is That Doggie in the Window? (backwards)

Window the in doggie
That is much how
Tail waggly
The with one the
Window the in doggie
That is much how
Sale for doggie's
That hope do I.

Once you've mastered this and wowed your friends, think how impressed they'd be if you learned something really complicated backwards – like a rap or the Swedish national anthem!

Tell a fortune with a Frazzle

Buy a bag of Frazzles (or similar bacon-themed expanded corn snack). Or, better still, get your mum to buy you a bag of Frazzles. You can be subtle about this – drop hints like: "You know what I fancy, Mum? A bag of Frazzles!" or "I tell you what would go nicely with this tomato soup, Mum – a Frazzle." If that fails, just stand at the front door and scream, "I WANT A FRAZZLE!"

Get an envelope. You can always re-use an old envelope and cover up the address and stamp with some paper.

Write "Miracle Frazzle" on the front of the envelope – ideally in red pen – and draw as best you can a picture of ... er ... a Frazzle.

I think if there is a prize for the most mentions of the word "Frazzle" in a book, I might win it!*

On the other side of the envelope, write a list of predictions. You can make up your own or use these:

Frazzle Curls Up at Both Ends	Shy, would suit job in Hotel Management
Frazzle Curls Up at One End	Extrovert, good fun to be with, but you wouldn't want to be trapped in a lift with them
Frazzle Stands on Its End	Very highly strung
Frazzle Remains Flat	Gullible!

Go up to a friend and explain that you have a miracle Frazzle that can predict what sort of person they are. Ask them to put their hand out flat and then place the Frazzle on the upturned palm. Wait a little while and then say, "Hmm, remains flat... Let's see what that means..."

Consult the back of the envelope and then tell them, "Gullible!"

* Actually, the most mentions of the word "Frazzle" can be found in *The Observer Book of Frazzles*, published by Hachette.

DAY 245

Make sculptures from void fill

OK, I know what you're thinking: "What the blinking heck is void fill?" Well, it's the technical term for those Wotsit-shaped pellets you get packed around fragile stuff that gets delivered to your house. Yes, I agree it's rather a depressing name. I'd much rather call them Fun Puffs or Puffy Lumps.

So (and here's the big news) one day I discovered that if you lick the ends of these things, they become sticky and if you press two together they stick and you can make sculptures out of them. Basically, it's a free Lego set!

I'm not suggesting you lick them – they might be toxic after all. Use a damp sponge instead of your tongue (actually that's good advice for life!).

You can make all sorts of things – animals, necklaces, buildings, words, why even whole cities – and it's absolutely FREE! PLUS, they make great Christmas presents for family and friends! Well, OK, not GREAT Christmas presents, but definitely CHEAP Christmas presents – the sort of thing you could get away with giving to your nan.

Here are some of the things I've made:

1. Bangle

2. Cube

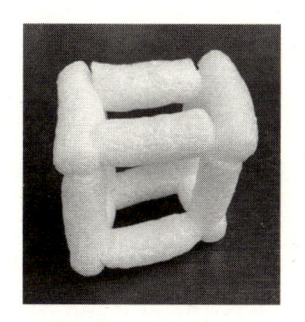

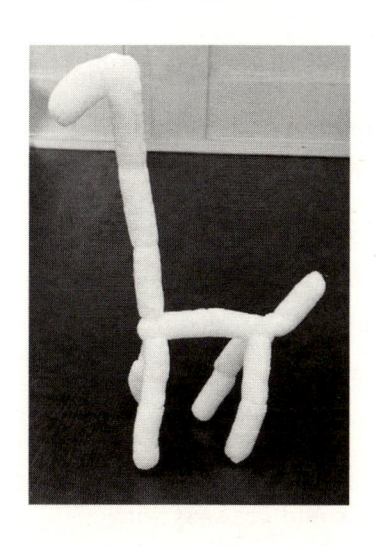

3. Giraffe

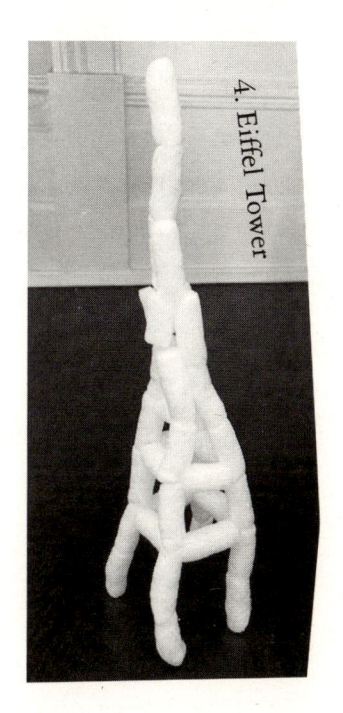

4. Eiffel Tower

5. Geodesic dome
(Ooops! Sorry, I haven't finished that one yet!)

Do everything backwards for a day

Put your clothes on back to front – this is pretty achievable, although the shoes might pose a problem.

Walk backwards – make sure you hold on to the banister going downstairs, and if you're walking along the street, make sure you've got someone with you to guide you. It would be very embarrassing if you were run over by a car with your clothes on back to front. The paramedics might try and twist your head round so it's facing the right way.

Try speaking backwards – so instead of saying "Hi! How are you today? Lovely weather we're having for this time of year", you'd say "Year of time this for having we're weather lovely. Today you are how, Hi?"

It's good to maybe work out what you're going to say backwards before you say it. Here are some useful phrases – see if you can work out what they mean:

* "Toilet public a to me direct you can me excuse?"
* "Centre city the for bus correct the this is?"
* "Dog the worming was I because night last homework my do to able wasn't I sir sorry I'm."
* "Ball foot of game a for park the over going fancy you do?"
* "That watching not I'm *Show Road Antiques* it's, no oh!"

DAY 247

Use yourself as a printing press

I think we already mentioned the artist Yves Klein, who covered his friends in paint and got them to roll around on a big piece of paper to make a sort of painting. Well, most of us don't have those sorts of friends, but you can have a go with your arms and legs!

Try making a painting by putting washable poster paint on your fingers, hands, knees, elbows – but not necessarily all at once.* Turn these prints into animals, people, creatures by adding arms and legs and faces.

Fingerprint   Elbowprint

After the paint has dried, stick 'em in your scrapbook.

⚠ * Wear an apron so you don't get paint on your clothes!

DAY 248

Paint a toilet roll portrait

Draw or paint a picture of your favourite toilet roll. Really spend some time on it so you do it justice. Make a cardboard frame for it and give it to your mum as a present.

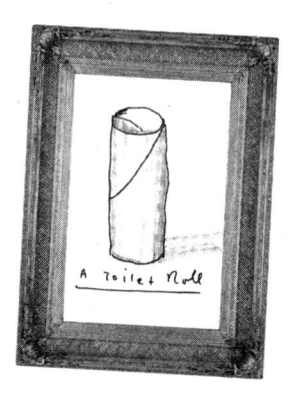

DAY 249

Lose yourself in the ball pool

Put a red, blue or yellow swimming hat on and see how long you can hide in the ball pool at your local IKEA store or soft play area.

WHERE'S HARRY?

DAY 250

Adopt a conker

A conker is the brown shiny nut that grows on the horse chestnut tree (Latin name: *Canni havmeconker*). No one seems to play conkers any more, which means loadsa conkers lying around doing nothing for us to find uses for.

Get a piece of string, about a metre long, and ask your pet adult to make a hole in a conker.

Thread the conker onto the piece of string and tie a big knot so it can't escape. Then, whenever you go anywhere, drag your conker around with you. Say things to the conker like "Come on, boy!" and let him sniff a lamppost if he wants to.

DAY 251

Hold conker trials

Re-thread your conker with a longer piece of string – maybe two metres this time. Tie the end of the string to the back of your bike. Tow the conker around off the back of your bike and see how long it takes to get worn down to nothing.

Then try the same thing with ...

* An apple
* A tomato
* A bread roll
* A coconut

Make a graph of your readings and send it to an important scientific journal like *Nature* or *New Scientist*. It'll probably take a while for them to get back to you, but when they do, I'd love to know what they say!

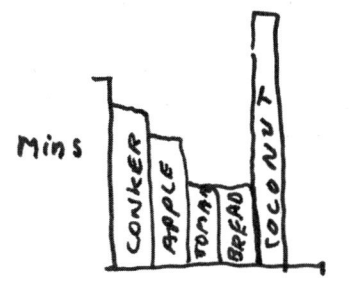

DAY 252
Make friends with a bald person

Make a tiny "CAUTION: UNEVEN SURFACE!" sign and put it on your dad's bald head while he's sleeping. Maybe you can think of some other silly places to put it?

NOTE

If your dad's not bald yet, just wait a while – he will be!

DAY 253
Hairbrush security device

Security is SO important, isn't it? Use a hairbrush as a hand-held metal detector like the ones they have at the airport.

As you pass the hairbrush over your dad's trouser pocket, make a bleeping sound and ask him to empty it into a tray. This doesn't actually detect anything potentially dangerous, but it certainly makes people think twice!

DAY 254

Send out an SOS

If you're stranded on a desert island and write a note asking for help, seal it up in a bottle then throw it in the sea, legend has it, it'll get washed ashore, someone will find it and then come and rescue you. Fat chance!

It's still quite a fun thing to do, though! Think of some funny messages you could put in bottles, and use the sea to deliver them. Here are some I've come up with:

> Help! I'm a bottle and I'm lost!

> Can you direct me to the nearest branch of Waitrose please?

> Help! I'm drowning! Love from the Milkman

> Calling all dolphins! I need a lift to the nearest dolphin dance party. I've got the moves; you bring the waves!

> Greetings, fishy friends! If you're reading this, you're now part of my underwater book club. Our first pick is *The Little Mermaid*.

DAY 255

Make a silly jigsaw

Next time someone breaks a china mug, ask an adult to put it in a shoe box and give it to your friend as a present. Tell them it's a "Mug Kit".

Write on the box "Glue not included" and don't include any glue. You could put a drawing of what the mug's supposed to look like on the front of the box to help them out though.

DAY 256

Make your own mutant dominoes

Make your own dominoes out of thick cardboard, painted black, then add as many white dots as you like! It's mutant dominoes!

DAY 257

Write a silly movie

With the rise of the smartphone and iPad and various apps for editing and adding music, it's never been easier for you and your friends to get together and make a movie!

A very silly movie, please.

It doesn't have to be long – in fact, in many ways you're better off cramming a lot into a small amount of time. Why not aim for three minutes?

Think of a story – or if you can't think of one, remake a three-minute version of your favourite film, or create a new film for an established film franchise. Use locations that are easy to get to – you could even make a new James Bond film in your house!

Here are some suggestions:

* **Quantum of Sofa** – a James Bond film about trying to find the best place to put the couch

* **Harry Potter and the Philosopher's Scone** – in which young wizard Harry Potter (played by … er … you) tries to make some scones for a visiting philosopher (played by your friend)

When writing your script, it's really important to keep the surprises coming. Here are a few ideas for a script for a film I'm calling *Indiana Jones and the Raiders of the Larg Fridge*. Maybe you've got a better idea for an ending?

SCENE 1: BEDROOM, INDIANA JONES'S HOUSE

Ageing adventurer Indiana Jones wakes up in the middle of the night and fancies a snack – but first he has to overcome a series of obstacles before he can get to the fridge.

Gasp as he thinks there's an intruder in the house ... and tries to fight him off before realizing he's looking in a full-length mirror and he's actually fighting himself!

Thrill as he hears the clanking and groaning sounds of a ghost coming from the airing cupboard ... only to find it's the hot-water tank that needs a service.

Then, horror of horrors, he sees a pair of hands sticking out from the bottom of the curtains. He punches the curtains ... and hurts his hand. There's no one behind them, just a pair of hands made from plaster.

When finally he makes it to the kitchen, he reaches for the fridge and swings open the door ... only to discover...

Here are a few possible endings:

- It's completely empty except for a note that says, "Sorry I ate all your food. Love, Grandma Jones".
- There's an empty fridge and a mouse – Indiana screams and runs off.
- As he opens the door, a hand comes out and punches him in the face.

DAY 258

Draw storyboards for your film

Once you've written your script – or adapted mine – make sure it's got a beginning, middle and sort of end.

Spend some time drawing out a few frames from each scene – so you know what you're doing when you come to make the film. This is called a storyboard.

DAY 259

Produce your film

Plan the making of your silly film. Write out a list of all the things you'll need and have to do before you make it. Things like: where you're going to film all the scenes, how you'll find the costumes and wigs, and who will do the make-up. Get costumes from charity shops or by raiding your family's wardrobe. Go through the list and get all these jobs done. This is called producing the film.

DAYS 260 AND 261

Shoot your movie!

Having done all that preparation, you're ready to make your film! It'll take you a day or two to film it and a day to edit all the bits together. Don't forget music and sound effects as they can really lift an otherwise dull scene.

SILLY FACT NUMBER 18

You never see cats on the beach. Why? Not sure. You'd think they'd like to hang out on the beach as they like eating fish and the sea is where the fish hang out, which is right next to the beach. But they don't, so what's going on? Let me know if you have any idea why cats refuse to go to the beach.

Coming to the beach, Stouffer?

NO!

DAY 262

Invite people to your movie premiere

Design and send out invitations to the world premiere of your movie. You might like to state how you'd like people to dress. Dress code: VERY SILLY! Or you could ask them to come dressed in the style of the movie you've made.

DAY 263

Hold a movie premiere

It's the big day! Screen your new movie on the largest TV screen you can get your hands on.

To make it even more special, get a couple of best friends to dress up as security guards – to prevent the wrong sort of people coming. Maybe even film people being interviewed as they arrive – this could form part of your next film.

Serve fizzy drinks and popcorn or, if you can't get those, water and biscuits! You might like to do a little speech before the film starts, where you thank everyone involved. But keep it short – you don't want to send the audience off to sleep before they've seen the movie.

provide drinks + snacks

DAY 264

Give yourself a new skin condition

Get a couple of Rice Krispies. Lick them and stick them onto your face. Ask your mum to book you an appointment to see a skin expert as you've grown a wart.

I'm a Rice krispie!

Maybe you need some moisturizer?

DAY 265

Make some splat paintings

Hang a piece of white paper on an outside wall or a tree – or place it on a patch of grass. Fill an old sock with mud and swing it round your head a couple of times before whacking it onto the piece of paper. Make sure you do this outside.

Not only do these socks make a very interesting pattern on the paper – but it's also enormously satisfying! Once they're dry, these splat paintings make great gifts!

DAY 266

Make a flip-flop shy

Get a friend to lie on their back without any shoes and socks on and put their feet up in the air. Then throw flip-flops at their feet to see if you can get them to stay on.

Take it in turns to be the thrower and the feet – before you know it, it'll be lunchtime!

DAY 267

Talk in raspberries

Have a conversation with a friend, but instead of words, just blow raspberries. Write down what you think the friend was saying and get them to write down what they thought you were saying, then compare notes! Possible conversation:

YOU: Raaasp-raasp! (Hello!)

FRIEND: Rasp raaaaasp! (Hi there!)

YOU: Ra-rara ra ra ra-rasp? (What are you up to today?)

FRIEND: Rasp rarrassp ra. Rasp rar. Raaaaaasppp! Ra ra raraaasp rraaaaaaaasp? (I'm going to see my nan! Do you want to come too?)

YOU: Ra raaaasp! (No thanks!)

DAY 268

Play a game of giant football

Try playing football with a 1.5 m-wide weather balloon instead of a regular football. If you can't get a weather balloon, try a regular balloon filled with water – or better still, custard.

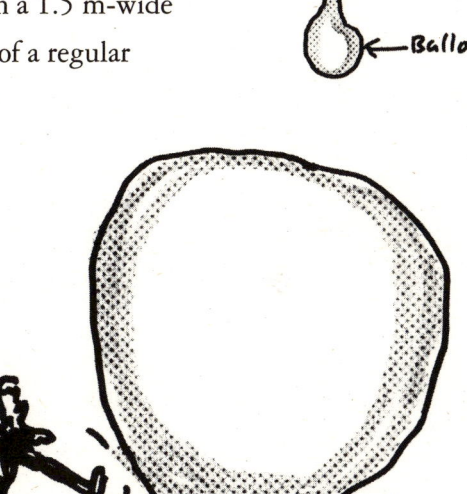

DAY 269

Help nature

Pop a roll of toilet paper on the end of a branch and put a sign next to it that says: "FOR SQUIRREL USE ONLY". Or try the same thing next to a statue, only change "squirrel" to "seagull".

DAY 270

Hold a lavish celebration of something really quite dull

Why should we only celebrate the big things in life like birthdays, weddings, graduating from university and winning the lottery?

Life's for living, after all! So let's celebrate the little things that normally go unmarked. Next time your mum goes down the shops, make a banner that says: "Congratulations on going down the shops, Mum!"

Or, when your dad gets his hair cut, make him a "Love the new haircut!" greetings card. Or throw a party to celebrate Bin Day.

I'm sure you'll have some ideas of your own for this challenge.

DAY 271

Perform two-dimensional plastic surgery

You can do a version of plastic surgery on a photo of a celebrity cut from a magazine. Take the photo, snip bits out with a pair of scissors and glue them back together onto another piece of paper.

Watch the years peel away!

BEFORE   AFTER

DAY 272

Work out the shortest route

Make your own silly A to B or C game. Here's mine:

Harry loves coffee and doughnuts but hates doing the washing-up – so show him the shortest way to get to his coffee and doughnut and avoid the washing-up!

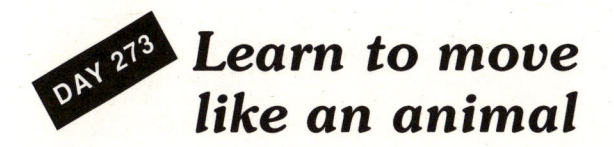

DAY 273

Learn to move like an animal

As you see a dog walking down the street, copy its walk. Go to the park and act like a squirrel; mingle with the ducks at the duck pond by acting like them. Pretty soon you'll be a regular Mowgli!*

* *The Jungle Book* reference!

DAY 274

Stage a bun fight

BREAD ROLL   SNOWBALL
              (partially melted)

We all love a snowball fight, but let's face it, it hardly EVER snows except in places like Lapland, Alaska and Scotland. Here's how you have all the fun of a snowball fight without getting cold and wet. Instead of snowballs, use bread rolls, buns and baps! I know, I know, I can just hear your mum and dad saying, "You can't waste good baps on such a silly idea!" Don't worry, I'm suggesting you use stale buns, baps and rolls. Go along to the bakers at the end of the day and show them this message:

Dear Baker,

My friend here is organizing a bread fight – it's like a snowball fight only with bread. Please supply them with any spare bread rolls. They can be stale. Anything you've got, basically. I promise they're not going to set up a rival bakery across the road.

Thanks!
Luv n stuff
Francis Hill x

President – The Royal Order of Upside-Down Snow Ferrets

At the end of the fight, MAKE SURE YOU PICK UP ALL THE BUNS AND PUT THEM IN THE BIN or you'll be fighting off ducks closely followed by rats!

DAY 275

Make a welcome mat for a bird table

If you want to attract exotic and interesting birds to your bird table, it's important they feel right at home, so let's make a welcome mat for a bird table.

It doesn't have to be anything fancy – just a rectangle of fabric with some words of welcome written on it in black marker pen. You might just write "WELCOME", or you might prefer to go for something more jokey like "Welcome to my crib". You could even write "WELCOME" in bird language, which is "Twiddley dee-dee dee twiddle twiddle twiddle" (which is a bit long, which is why birds hardly ever have welcome mats – it doesn't help that they can't write either … or hold a pen).

DAY 276

Become a litter monster

Get some old clothes, or, even better, get hold of one of those disposable bodysuits that painters and decorators wear, attach all kinds of litter to it – stuff like milk cartons, cardboard and plastic wrapping, plastic bottles etc.*

Make sure you wash them out first or you'll really stink (that's a different monster!**) then wander around going, "Raaaar!*** I'm the litter monster! Gimme your litter!"

Carry a black bin liner with you. It's actually a really good, community-minded way of keeping your area clean. Pretty soon, you'll hear people saying things like: "Wow! The streets are so clean! Thank you, Litter Monster!"

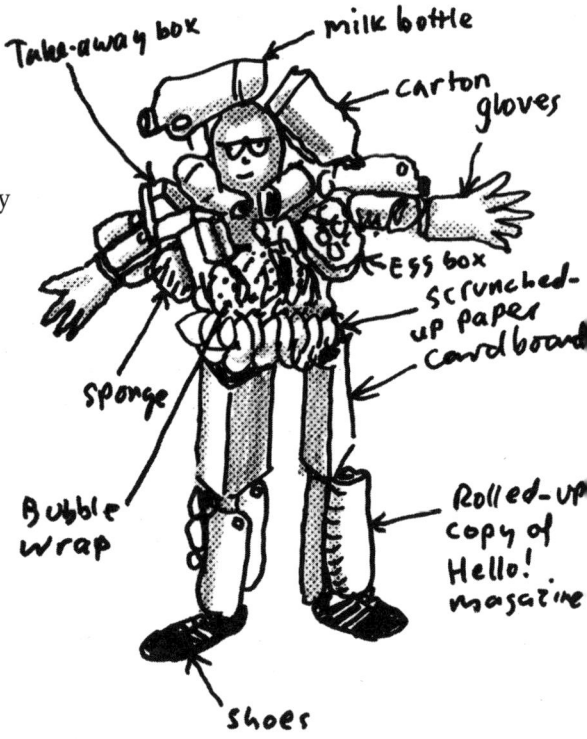

Labels on illustration: Take-away box, milk bottle, carton, gloves, Egg box, scrunched-up paper, cardboard, sponge, Bubble wrap, Rolled-up copy of Hello! magazine, shoes

---

* Be careful picking up litter – don't touch anything sharp or stinky!

** That's Stinky the Stink Monster.

*** Not to be confused with the noise the Plain Naan Monster makes, which is "NAAAAAAAAAN!"

DAY 277

Create a new species

In the Middle Ages, they used to serve a weird dish at banquets – made up of the top half of a pig attached to the bottom half of a turkey. (Yuck! I think I'm going to be sick). It was called a cockentrice.

Why not design some combi-animals of your own?
A half fish, half cat – or fishcat – or a half dog, half bat – or dogbat – or a half goat, half zebra – or gobra.

Make sure you draw them and stick them in your silly scrapbook.

Duck Harry

Swan Harry

Duck Horse

Duck Pig

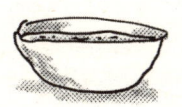

Duck soup

I'm an owl!

DAY 278

Owl Boy & the Amazing Revolving Head Trick

Ever wanted to make like an owl and revolve your head almost 360 degrees? Me too! Well, here's how!

You'll need a cardboard box that fits neatly over your head. If you can't get one the right size, just adapt whatever box you can find.

On one side, cut a fairly narrow letter-box-style window for your eyes: PLEASE DON'T TRY TO MAKE THE HOLE WHILE YOU'RE WEARING IT OR YOU MAY END UP CUTTING YOUR NOSE OFF AND POKING YOUR EYES OUT! And it'll be me that gets the blame.

Take the box off your head first. Be sure not to make the hole too big, or it'll spoil the effect. Better to start with a hole that's too small that you can make bigger than one that's too big and then have to start all over again.

You might like to decorate the box with "The Amazing OWL BOY" or "OWL GIRL" or "OWL PERSON" or even paint it to look like an owl – maybe collect some feathers and stick those on, or go to the woods and see if a real owl will let you borrow theirs.

To achieve the trick requires a little bit of practice...

Place the box over your head so you're looking out of the hole – then slowly turn the box round – turning your head at the same time, so it goes round with the box. Unless your parents are owls, you'll only be able to turn your head about 90 degrees in either direction – so once your head has reached its turning limit, turn it back the other way so it's facing 90 degrees in the opposite direction (this will be hidden from view because the window in the box is now facing backwards). Keep rotating the box until the window comes round to meet your face, and then join it for the last bit so it's facing the front. To anyone standing in front of you, it looks like you've just rotated your head a full 360 degrees!

Like a lot of magic tricks, a big part of whether it's convincing is the way you sell it to the viewer. So, as you're revolving your head, you might like to make some noises like it's really hurting. Stuff like: "Argh! My neck!"

Sounds complicated right? It's not really – it's just tricky to explain. Here's a diagram:

Here's a video of me doing it...

Excuse me? How far to the beach?

← noodle

Long walk to the beach

DAY 279

Walk around in a diving mask, snorkel and flippers and ask the first person you see for directions to the beach. When they say, "I'm sorry, there is no beach near here..." say, "That's Airbnb for you!"

I don't tend to hang out at the beach!

DAY 280

Do some cereal experiments

Connect two pipe cleaners to a smiley potato, then press these wires to each end of a Rice Krispie and jot down what happens.

* Nothing
* Explosion
* Comes alive

Mmm, that feels nice!

— Rice krispie

Then try it with a sugar puff. Compare your results.

Make a note of your findings in your scrapbook.

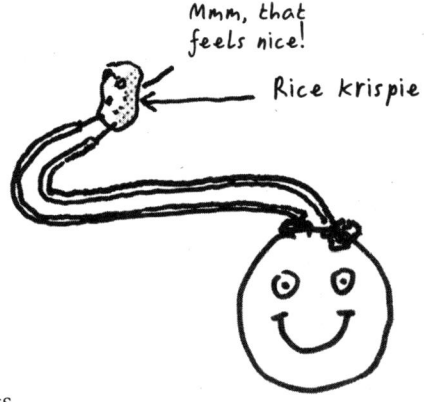

DAY 281

Act like a crustacean

Tie an empty cardboard box onto your back with some string. Walk sideways everywhere. If anyone asks what you're doing, tell them, "I'm trying to find out how it feels to be a crab." Then try and pinch them.

Now I'm a crab!

Make a car-based disguise

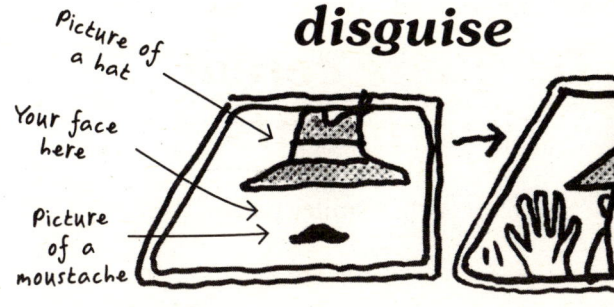

DAY 282

Picture of a hat
Your face here
Picture of a moustache

Draw a picture of a hat and a moustache – make them full-sized so they would fit on your head. Colour them in and make them as lifelike as possible.

Then stick them on the inside of your car window so the design is facing outwards. Not the windscreen, though, as your designated driver might not be able to see out!

Place them at a height so that when you're looking out of the window, it looks like you've got a moustache and are wearing a hat. Wave at people in other cars as you pass them, and watch them smile!

DAY 283

Go cycling in the sky

Try cycling a bike upside down. Go outside, lie on your back with the bike on top of you and pretend you're cycling through the sky.

DAY 284

Read a bedtime story to a pet

Read a bedtime story to a pet. Change all the characters to animals that the pet might recognize. So, if you're reading *Goldilocks and the Three Bears* to a hamster, make Goldilocks a hamster rather than a little girl, and make the bears – dunno ... maybe dogs?

Once upon a time, there was a cat ... called ... Cinderella...

DAY 285

Hold a birthday party for a butterfly

Thimble full of sugary water

Butterflies are not terribly sociable insects, are they? You rarely see whole gangs of butterflies hanging out like you do with bees or wasps. Maybe it's because they're shy and need a bit of help meeting other butterflies? That's why I'm suggesting you hold a butterfly party.

Write out tiny invitations and leave them around places that butterflies like to go to – like flower beds.

Think about what food butterflies like to eat and prepare them tiny snacks and drinks.

What kind of music do you think butterflies like to listen to? Maybe "Build Me Up Buttercup", or "Butterflyz" by Alicia Keyes, or "Kiss from a Rose" by Seal, or "Daisies" by Katy Perry?

What kind of party games do butterflies enjoy? Pin the Sting on the Bee? Nectar-sip challenge?

NOTE
If not many butterflies turn up to the party, check that your invitations had all the details.

DAY 286

Invent something seriously silly

It's all very well coming up with brilliant life-changing inventions like the cordless vacuum cleaner and the telescopic shoe horn, but how about some silly inventions for a change? So, come up with the silliest inventions you can think of. Here are two of mine to start you off:

* **The Harmonistache** – Isn't it annoying when your moustache gets stuck in your harmonica? Look no further than the Harmonistache – a harmonica with built-in moustache.

* **The Wi-Fi Toaster** – A toaster that connects to the internet and prints your tweets or emails onto your toast. Breakfast just got a lot more informative!

Send your ideas into Dragons' Den, BBC TV. Here are some ACTUAL SILLY INVENTIONS THAT GOT MADE!!

Silly inventions

* **The Alarm Clock That Runs Away**
  An alarm clock on wheels that rolls away from your bedside table every morning, forcing you to chase it to turn it off.

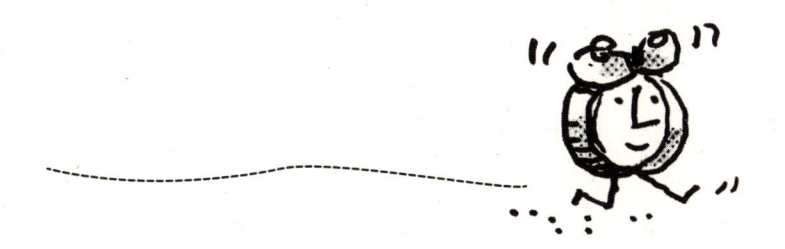

* **The Baby-Mop Onesie**
  Turn your baby into a tiny cleaning machine. This onesie has mop-like material on the underside, so as your baby crawls, they polish the floor.

* **Ice-Cream Cone Rotator**
  Licking an ice cream is such a hassle, isn't it? Not any more, thanks to the rotating cone that will move the ice cream so you can leave your tongue in one place.

DAY 287

Create a flume for a doll

Remember the biscuit delivery system that you made on **Day 154**? I hope you didn't throw it away! Today it's going to become a flume for a very small doll (like the ones in a doll's house). Get hold of a plastic container like you get takeaway food in, paint the inside of it blue and fill it with water so it looks like a swimming pool.

Place the water-filled container under the opening of the cardboard tube and release the doll into the upper end. Make sure you give the doll a little mat to ride down on to avoid chafing!

small dolly
Toilet roll FLUME
Take-away tray or Tupperware Box painted blue
water

SILLY PEOPLE Nº 3

Composer John Cage once released a piece of music called 4'33", which was basically four minutes and thirty-three seconds of silence – the performer does absolutely nothing!

JOHN GAGE

DAY 288

Make a jet-propelled desk chair

Sit on a desk chair with a leaf blower pointing to one side and turn it on.* OMG! You got yourself a revolving chair!

This works much better with a rechargeable leaf blower, of course – otherwise the wire gets tangled. With a rechargeable one, the world's your oyster! I once travelled all the way from London to Exeter in my chair; mind you, it took me a year and a half, but I made so many new friends.

BUT

(and it's a big but) do this indoors and stop if you get dizzy!

HAS ANYONE SEEN MY LEAF BLOWER?

* You don't need a big or heavy leaf blower – just a small rechargeable one – and make sure you have your pet adult on hand for this one, just in case!

269

DAY 289

Let's play Celebrity Bushes

Point at a bush and say, "Oh look, it's… [insert the name of a celebrity]! So it might be: "Oh look, it's Adele in a bush!" or "Oh look, it's Stormzy! What's he doing in a bush?" or "Oh look, it's Former Labour Health Secretary, Alan Milburn! Hiding in a bush of all places."

You'll be surprised at just how many people turn around and try to see if they can see them too!

Hey! It's PAUL HOLLYWOOD!

PAUL! PAUL! PAUL!

Adrian Serious's wife

DAY 290

Teach a stick to swim

Take a stick down to the duck pond and teach it to swim. You might like to give it a few lessons in your bath first, just to give it a bit of confidence. Make sure you take a towel so the stick doesn't catch cold.

BREATHE!

DAY 291

Encourage a woodlouse

Nobody loves me...

Life can be hard, especially if you're a woodlouse – spending all your time scurrying around in the dark and damp looking for wood to eat and worried about drying out – so let's give woodlice a bit of encouragement.

Lift a small pot plant, stone or an old log, the sort of places woodlice like to hang out, and shout encouraging things to them – you know, things to make them feel good about themselves. Stuff like:

* "Hey! Look at you! You're doing so well!"
* "Proud of you guys!"
* "You got this, Woody. Stay focused!"
* "You've got to learn to love yourself before you can love another louse!"

Make sure you put the pot, stone or log back down afterwards or they'll dry out and that'll be completely counterproductive.

A stone

DAY 292

Start a school for cats

Cats do the dumbest things, right? Is it any wonder when they're not actually receiving any formal teaching? That's why I'm suggesting setting up a school for cats. Come up with a suitable name for it – I've called mine St Kit's School for Cats.

* Have a think about what type of lessons cats might enjoy and benefit from. At my cat school I'm teaching:
  * **Cat History** (literally the history of cats)
  * **Cat Biology** (that's biology for cats, not just about cats)
  * **Cat Art** – art by cats and of cats
  * **Cat PE** (turns out, cats love badminton!)
* Draw a plan of the school with all the different areas that would be required – play area, toilets, scratching area.
* Draw up a timetable.
* Ask local cats to enroll in the school.
* Write report cards for your cat pupils – otherwise, if there's no feedback, how will they know where their weaknesses lie?

HEY! STOUFFER! Shouldn't you be in class?

I'm 32 years old, HARRY!

DAY 293

Pretend you got run over

Before   After   I'm so tyre-d

Ask the designated driver in your house whether you can borrow the spare tyre from the car. If they say "No!", keep asking them over and over until you wear them down – that's the driver, not the tyre!

Ask the driver to help you take the tyre and paint the tread – that's the bit that is in contact with the road – with brown poster paint, then take an old white shirt or T-shirt and roll the tyre over it. When the paint is dry, put the shirt on and run indoors shouting, "I've been run over!"

Make sure you rinse the tyre off afterwards, or I'll get the blame, and I get enough letters of complaint as it is!

DAY 294

Plane spotting

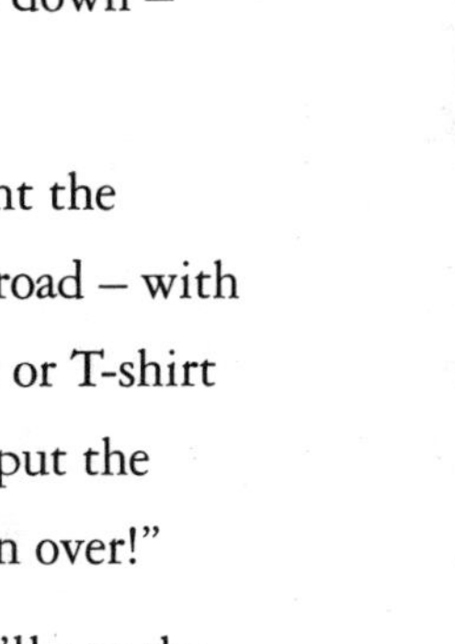

SQUAWK!

Metal bird!

When a plane flies over, point up into the sky and shout, "Metal bird! Metal bird!"

DAY 295

Magic travelcard fun

If you live in a big city like London, Birmingham or Swaffham, you'll need a pass to get around on the trains and the buses. To get through the barriers you simply touch your pass on the sensor and they open up, allowing you through. There's a bit of fun to be had, though.

Get a photo of your nan (or anyone at all really – it could even be a photo of your dog) and tuck the travelcard behind it so it's hidden. Approach the barrier and touch the photo of Nan on the sensor and watch as everyone around you is amazed as it opens up. As you walk through the barrier, say "Thanks, Nan!" and give the photo a big kiss.

SILLY FACT NUMBER 111,000

At the age of just three months, an elephant's tusks fit exactly into the holes of a standard French electric plug socket. This is why there are no elephants younger than four months allowed in France.

DAY 296

Develop a silly phobia

Pretend you have an irrational fear of something silly, like multi-storey car parks. When you see one, scream:

"Aaagh! Multi-storey car park!"

and

"My eyes are burning! Take me away from here!"

and

"No one comes out of the multi-storey car park alive!!!" and other stuff along those lines.

DAY 297

Make a phobia map

Write a list of all the multi-storey car parks you've been to or seen and their locations so you can avoid them in future. Maybe take some photos or draw them and rank them in order of how scary they are.

DAY 298

Make a pair of spooky hands

Fill a pair of rubber gloves with plaster of Paris (plaster of Paris is great stuff – you can get it from the art shop or, I'm going to say it again ... ONLINE!).

Get your pet adult to help you as it's tricky, messy stuff to work with.

SPOOKY HANDS

I'VE CHANGED MY MIND!

Once the plaster has set – which will take at least twenty-four hours – carefully peel or cut off the rubber gloves so that you've now got two plaster hands.

Leave them to properly dry out and harden somewhere warm like an airing cupboard or on a radiator, then paint them (regular poster paint works fine). You might like to make them as lifelike as you can, or you might prefer to paint them green and turn them into "zombie hands".

Leave the hands in various places and see how people react.

Suggested places:

* Sticking up out of a flower bed! Like someone was buried but has changed their mind!

* Sticking out from under your mum's bed – like someone's hiding under it!

* In the fridge – yuck!

DAY 299

Create a spooky graveyard

INSERT NAME HERE

Make some mini gravestones out of cardboard. Write some funny epitaphs (funny words written on graves). Here are some of my favourites…

I TOLD YOU I WAS ILL

BEST BEFORE 1ST OCTOBER 1888…

I WILL NOT BE RIGHT BACK AFTER THIS MESSAGE

SHE ALWAYS SAID HER FEET WERE KILLING HER, BUT NO ONE BELIEVED HER

WOW! IT'S DARK DOWN HERE

HERE LIES GOOD OLD FRED. A GREAT BIG ROCK FELL ON HIS HEAD

DAY 300

Celebrity Mexican wrestling

Find out what celebrities would look like as Mexican wrestlers by painting Mexican "lucha libre" wrestling masks on top of photos of them.

Cut out some pictures of your favourite celebs, politicians or members of the Royal Family. Take a piece of tracing paper and trace the outline of each celebrity's head, eyes, nose and mouth. Draw your mask onto the tracing paper and cut out holes for the eyes, nose and mouth. There are lots of different designs – all brightly coloured – take a look on the internet. Here are a few classics.

EL STORMZY

KIDZOE BALL

Los Hazza

TINY TEMPAH

LOS SERIOUS

Add colour to the mask with poster paints. You might like to give your celebrity wrestler a racy wrestler's name like "El Gangster", "Hombre Southgate" or "Kid Fiona Bruce".

DAY 301

Let's wrestle!

Make a poster advertising a celebrity wrestling match using the pictures you made yesterday. Write a couple of lines to describe the wrestlers' styles – things like "El Rylan – he's good, but he can certainly be bad when it's called for!" or "Hombre Southgate, the Wizard from Watford – gonna make his ancestors proud!"

LOS SERIOUS

He's not messing around (he hates that)

DAY 302

Play Bread Snap!

Play snap with a loaf of sliced bread. Maybe mix some brown bread in with the white to make it a little more exciting! When a matching piece of bread is put down, don't shout "snap!" shout "bap!"

DAY 303

Make a scary stocking mask

Get a pair of your mum's old stockings or tights – make sure she washes them first because you don't want to catch something, like athlete's foot of the face. Put the stocking over your head and look in a mirror.

Stocking face

Tights face

So far, so weird, right? Now, pull the end of the stocking up – as it travels up your face it takes the end of your nose and mouth with it, making you look even weirder. Put a hat on to hide the end of the stocking and lie on your back in the front room – or somewhere someone is sure to stumble across you. If you can, video their reaction, because, believe me, it'll be priceless!

Notey-note

Obvs make sure the tights aren't thick, otherwise you'll struggle to breathe!

DAY 304

Silly shadow puppets

Let's do some shadow puppets, but let's do them our way – the silly way. Everyone does the rabbit, the flying dove and the dog, but how about some slightly more unusual shadow puppets – I mean, every shadow deserves its chance to shine. I'm sure you'll have your own ideas, but here are a few of my favourites:

* The pebble
* The stick
* The hook
* The stain

Invite your family and friends to see your shadow puppets – what a great night out!

Ladies and gentlemen, I give you ...

THE PEBBLE!

DAY 305

Birthday present disguises

Some fruit pastilles wrapped to look like a guitar

A packet of chewing gum wrapped up to look like a doll's house

It's tricky handing over a present that is a bit small and unexciting-looking, isn't it? Never mind when people say, "The best presents come in small packages." Nonsense! I want big, fancy-looking presents, and I want them now! That's why it's a nice idea to wrap up the presents to look like something else.

Simply take the present — say a bar of soap, an ideal present for your little sister — and pad it out with cardboard and bubble wrap to make it look like a full-sized guitar. Or wrap up the packet of fruit pastilles you've bought your brother so it looks like a car.

It's quite a lot of work, but it's worth it just to see the face of the person you're giving the present to! Maybe try and get a before and after photo for your records.

DAY 306

Swap your life for someone else's

Fed up with seeing the world through the same eyes? Do you feel like the people you know have made their minds up about what you're like and what you like to do? Me too!

So, what's the answer? Well, why not be someone else for a day? (Or for the afternoon if you get up late.) Invent a WHOLE NEW CHARACTER! Give your new character a name, think about their backstory, where they're from – do they have an accent? What colour is their hair? What kind of person are they? That'll influence what kind of clothes they're wearing (you should be able to get some fairly cheap clothes from charity shops and car boot sales).

Does this person have any brothers or sisters, pets or enemies? Do they have a job? What are their hobbies? What kind of music or TV programmes do they like? Write all this stuff down so you can remember it. You could even make them a birth certificate or passport.

Then, once you've become this new person, wander around doing the sort of things you think they would like to do. Go to ASDA and buy the sort of sweets they would buy. Go to the park and play the sort of games they would play, introduce yourself as that person to people, friends and family. See how long you can keep it up for. It might actually make you appreciate who you really are!

Here's the person I like to pretend to be from time to time:

Name	Barry Bill
Description	age 45, thick black curly hair, beret and moustache
Occupation	works at the cheese factory putting the holes into the cheeses
Hobbies	pressing wild birds

Beret

Moustache

Barry Bill

DAY 307

Make out you've got a tiny head

Get a doll, balance it on top of your head, put a long coat on and do it up with just the doll's head poking out of the top (you might need an adult to help you safety pin the top of the coat). Make sure no one can see your face – but leave a small gap for you to see out of.

Walk around the streets and see how people react to a fully grown person with a doll's head.

If you can't get a doll, then a teddy bear might work too. Maybe try it with three legs like on **Day 51**!

DAY 308

Invent a conversation

What are you having for dinner? — *Sausages!*

You probably know the old joke, "What did one wall say to the other wall? I'll meet you in the corner!"

It's an interesting and very silly idea to wonder what things might say to each other if they could talk.

Draw a picture of two things and fill in the speech bubbles.

Here are some other ideas for conversations:

* Between two trees
* Between a car and a traffic light
* Between a fish and a lobster
* Between a dog and a lamppost
* Between a knife and fork
* Between a TV and a sofa

Where are you going on holiday? *Staycation.*

A bush minding its own business

287

DAY 309

See how many coats you can wear

How many coats can you put on one over the other? You might need to borrow some coats. Make a list of all the different coats and what order you put them on – just in case you have to do it again in a hurry. Put it in your scrapbook.

If you haven't got enough coats, try socks.

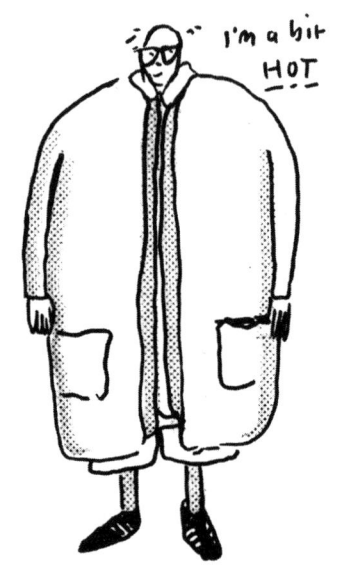

I'm a bit HOT

DAY 310

Email a pet

Set up an email account for a goldfish – something like georgethegoldfish@googlemail.com. Send him an email and see if he replies.

If you don't have a goldfish, set up an email address for another pet. If you don't have any pets, then set up an email for an imaginary pet.

DAY 311

Become a human Hoover

Tell your mum or dad that you're going to help clean up the front room. Then cover yourself in double-sided sticky tape and roll around on the carpet and soft furnishings* and see how much fluff you can pick up.

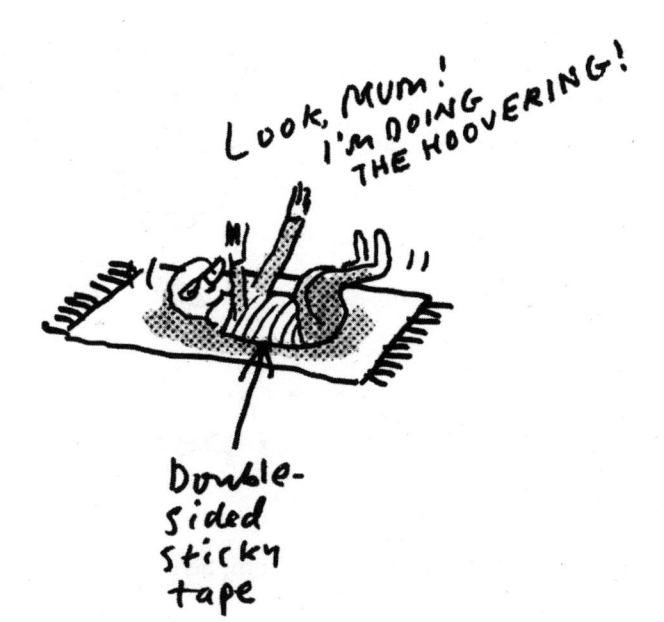

Look, mum! I'm doing the hoovering!

Double-sided sticky tape

* Er ... that's the sofa and armchairs to you!

SILLY FACT NUMBER 19
Hedgehogs and tortoises share some of the same interests – foraging for food, *The Chase* and anything with marzipan on it.

DAY 312

Make some warning snacks

Get a bag of tortilla chips and empty them into a bowl. Sort out all the whole ones and eat all the other bits. With an edible pen, taking care not to crack them, write messages on the chips warning of the dangers of eating triangular food.

Serve these to your family, then afterwards offer them some pieces of Dairylea cheese triangles or a piece of Toblerone. See if your warnings about triangular food have worked!

DAY 313

Hold the silliest birthday party ever!

Using the collage skills you learned on **Day 55**, put together a collaged photograph of an imaginary party! It might include David Beckham, Nelson Mandela, Ed Sheeran, Taylor Swift and Liz Truss! Stick it in your scrapbook!

Train your hamster to like a celeb

DAY 314

Today we're going to be training your hamster to like a particular celebrity, such as Alison Hammond or Dermot O'Leary. Every time you feed your hamster or give him or her a treat, wear a mask of the celebrity. You can make the mask by printing a photo of their face onto a piece of paper and cutting it out.

Before you know it, your hamster will be begging to watch anything with Alison or Dermot in it – *This Morning*, *Great British Bake Off* or *The Lottery* adverts.

NOTE:

It doesn't have to be a hamster – it could be your dog or cat or a local squirrel. And it doesn't have to be Alison or Dermot – it could be anyone who's regularly on TV, like Romesh Ranganathan or even Princess Anne.

DAY 315

Pretend you're a moth

Dress up as a moth and hide in your parents' wardrobe.

Make some wings out of brown paper or old wallpaper painted brown, put the stocking you had on **Day 303** over your head and use some swimming goggles for eyes. You're now ready to surprise them.

As they open the wardrobe doors, stumble out and if you can manage it, let out a big burp and say "Mmmmmm! Yum-yum! Nice clothes!" then run off.*

DAY 316

Upside-down national anthem

Lie upside down and whistle the national anthem. This is just a small act of rebellion, but you gotta start somewhere. For those readers in Australia – you're already doing this, so keep it up!

* Because moths eat clothes – you knew that, right?

DAY 317

Sleep down under

It's boring being asleep, isn't it? Here's how you can shake it up. Instead of sleeping ON your bed, sleep UNDER your bed. Take the bedding off and wedge it under the bed. You'll have to clear out all the stuff from under your bed first – all that stuff that you never use or has just fallen down there and got forgotten – but this might be a good chance to go through it and chuck it out.

When you wake up in the morning, try to remember you're under your bed, not on it, or you'll bang your head. It happened to me once, and I wrote this poem about it.

UNDER THE BED
By Harry Hill

I decided to slumber under my bed,
But when I awoke, I banged my head.
I thought for a moment that I was dead.
It left a bump, which went quite red,
So I cheered myself up with a piece of bread,
Covered in butter and chocolate spread.
Yum-yum!

DAY 318

Design a wanted poster for a mouse

Draw a picture of a mouse, give it a name and describe its crimes!

> # WANTED!
> ## IN FIVE COUNTIES
> ### Cheryl the Mouse
>
> CRIMES: Stealing cheese, nibbling one corner of a bag of muesli and leaving droppings behind the sofa
>
> REWARD:
> 1 POUND OF
> EXTRA-MATURE
> CHEDDAR CHEESE

(You'll need to decide what it's worth to you to catch Cheryl – the chances are you won't ever be able to be sure it's her you've caught, so you can probably afford to set it quite high.)

DAY 319

Arrange a mouse line-up

Imagine you've caught eight mice — one of which is Cheryl the Mouse, who is wanted in five counties for a number of crimes. Draw an identity parade of all the mice.

SILLYFACT №14

The flesh of the bumblebee is very nutritious and contains very high levels of vitamins — particularly vitamin B — hence the name.

Please don't eat me!

DAY 320

Play Litter Bingo

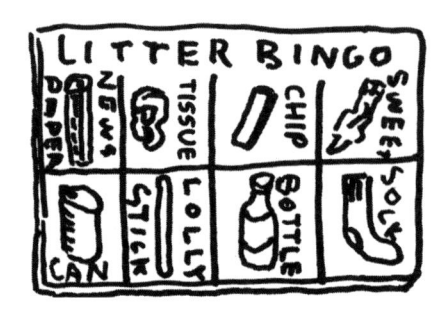

Here's a silly game to play when you're next on a walk to school, going to the shops or being taken to the police station for being too silly.

How to make the bingo cards:

Get some blank postcards. If you can't get those, use plain paper or old Christmas cards – just tear off the fronts and use the blank inside bit.

Divide the cards up into eight using a ruler or your dad's chin. In each rectangle draw a picture of an item of litter – a discarded bottle, some bubble wrap, an old sock, sweet wrappers, lolly stick, etc., and write underneath what it is.

Make sure you put some different items of litter on each bingo card, otherwise there'll be no clear winner. Obviously, it's more fun if you're walking with a couple of friends or your auntie and your cousins.

When you come across an item, cross it off on your card with a pencil or pen – the first person to get four in a row wins all the litter they've spotted!

DAY 321

Make a silly box of chocolates

The next time someone comes round to the house with a box of chocolates, keep the box and the empty trays after they've been eaten.

Replace the chocolates with a variety of weird and inedible objects like conkers, acorns, pebbles and bits of modelling clay,* and write a new guide to what they are.

* Obvs make sure no one eats them!

Caramel Conker
A salted caramel lump shaped to look like a conker.

Squirrel's Delight
Looks like an acorn, tastes quite acorny to be honest.

Mud Cluster
Handpicked mud ganache combined with grit for that earthy taste.

Bottle Top Surprise
Note the sticky residue around the outside of this brittle confectionery item.

Forever Pebble
Looks uncannily like a pebble, this treat is meant to last for ages on the tongue – possibly even forever.

Sticky Sensation Looks like a short piece of stick – because it is a short piece of stick! This treat is a great chew and is exceptionally high in fibre.

DAY 322

Design a sillymobile

Cars come with all sorts of extras these days – heated seats, heated steering wheels, phone chargers, TV screens – but what extras would you like to see in a car?

Maybe a passenger seat that ejects if the person sitting next to you is a bit boring (don't worry, there's a parachute to cushion their landing). How about a seat that converts into a toilet so you don't have to keep stopping for your little sister? How about a boot that doubles up as a jacuzzi? It's all to play for!

Draw your car as if it's an advert for a car in a magazine.

DAY 323

Let's play hide 'n' fruit

WHAT'S inside THE MELON?

Push a house key into an unpeeled satsuma – all the way in so it disappears completely – then ask your friend to peel it. When they discover the key, hold it up and say, "Is that your front door key?" You can do a similar thing with larger objects in bigger fruits:

* Grapefruit – pencil sharpener
* Cantaloupe melon – stapler
* Watermelon – torch

DAY 324

Play the new game of Hum-Shake

Shake your head and make a humming noise. I'm not sure why, but it's just kinda fun!

Humming noise

Spare humming noise that's broken away from the main group

Make a silly advent calender

I love Christmas, don't you? I particularly enjoy the build-up to Christmas and all its traditions like decorating the tree, arguing with my family, crying at the John Lewis advert on TV and of course opening the advent calendar.

But why be limited to the commercially available advent calendars with their corny pictures of donkeys and presents? How about an advent calendar tailored to suit someone you know? Well, here's how you can make your own advent calendar for next to nothing.

> **You'll need:**
> * Two pieces of card the same size – the front and back of a cereal packet will do it.
> * Scissors
> * Pencil
> * PVA glue

1. Draw twenty-four windows onto the unprinted side of one of the pieces of card, so that it looks like the front of an advent calendar.

2. Cut out the twenty-four windows. Don't cut all four sides out, though – remember one side acts as the window's hinge.

Windows

Pictures of stuff

3. Number these windows from 1–24.

4. Carefully open all the windows. Place the open-window card over the other piece of card and, using it as a stencil, mark with a pencil where the windows are.

5. Glue a photo, doodle or slogan onto each of the twenty-four spaces. Add stuff that will make your friend laugh – the famous poo emoji, a picture of the person they've got a crush on, or just pictures of yourself pulling funny faces.

6. Then glue just the edges of the piece of card with the windows so that it fits exactly over the piece of card with your secret visual treats. Try not to get glue on the windows, or the person you give it to will need a crowbar to open them.

7. Get your friends to make them too and swap 'em!

DAY 326

Cause a pile-up

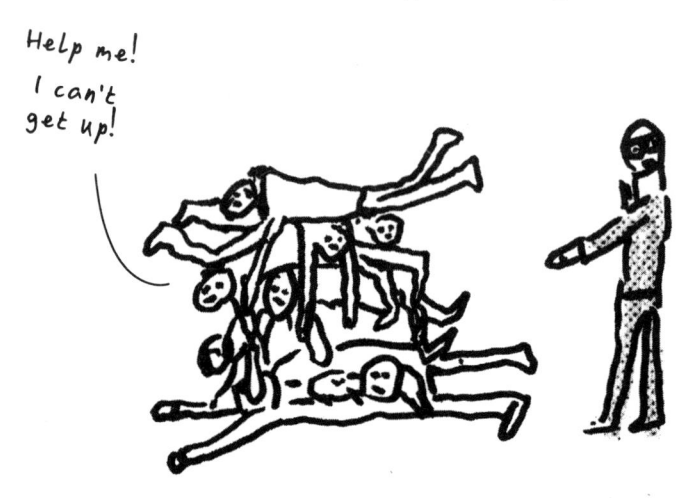

"Help me! I can't get up!"

Here's a very silly thing to do to cause a bit of a commotion — you need five or six friends or family members to help you.

Go to a fairly busy area like a shopping centre or cinema foyer and fall to the floor crying, "Help me! I can't get up!" Then put your hand up for help.

The next person tries to pull the first person up but gets pulled on top of them. They then put their hand up and repeat the plea for help: "Help me! I can't get up!"

The third person tries to help and gets pulled on top, then the fourth, then the fifth and so on. It ends up with you all rolling around on the floor until someone tells you to shove off!

Notey-note

Pile-ups are meant to be fun, but if it hurts, stop!

Learn some spoonerisms

A very silly chap called William Spooner was famous for the odd mistakes he made when he spoke. He'd get words, letters or sounds in a word mixed up so, for instance, "jelly beans" might become "belly jeans", and "Can I show you to another seat?" might become "Can I sew you to another sheet?"

These became known as "spoonerisms".

Here's some more:

* Roaring with pain – Pouring with rain
* Plaster man – Master plan
* Rental deceptionist – Dental receptionist
* Flock of bats – Block of flats
* Go and shake a tower – Go and take a shower
* Will nobody pat my hiccup? – Will nobody pick my hat up?

And here's a whole sentence packed with spoonerisms!

* The prandsome hince was just about to ask for Cinderella's mare in handage when the strock clarted to trike swelve.

I'd like you to come up with some new spoonerisms! Please let me know how you get on.

DAY 328

Make some bubblegum noses

Ever wondered how to have some fun with your bubblegum after you've chewed all the flavour out of it? Well, here's how: shape it to look like a nose and stick it on a photo of a celebrity over their nose so they now have a 3D nose.

DAY 329

Paint the back of the Mona Lisa

We all know the famous painting by Leonardo da Vinci called the *Mona Lisa*. Well, have you ever wondered what the back of her head looked like? Have a go at drawing or painting it. Maybe paint the back of some other famous scenes.

Mona Lisa (Top half)

Mona Lisa (Bottom half)

Yeah, she was wearing shorts and flip-flops. Well, she was sitting there for a long time so needed to be comfortable.

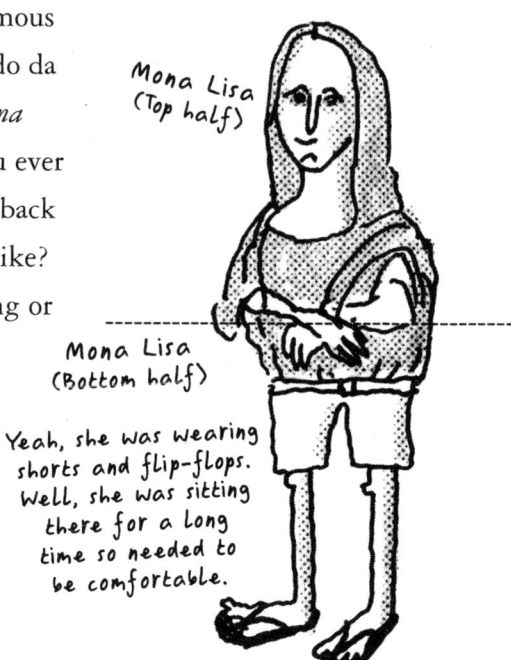

Poppycock!

DAY 330

(nice haircut btw)

Random compliments day

Great toast!

Thanks, Harry! I feel ready to face the day now.

Compliment items and objects around your house. Tell your toothbrush it's the best toothbrush ever or praise your toaster for its toasting abilities.

The toaster will feel good about itself – and, more importantly, so will you!

DAY 331

Make a banana – split

Next time you set off on a long journey, put a banana on the roof of your car and see how long it lasts before it falls off. Make a note of it. Next time, try peeling it first to see if that affects its ability to hold on.

Bananas

DAY 332

Go quackers!

Do a duck impression with two rice cakes. This is a really popular thing to do at parties – particularly at a duck party.

The best ones are the long rectangular rice cakes with the rounded edges, but any thin rice cakes will do. The thick ones are too heavy and don't work.

Lick your lips – you'll find the rice cakes stick to them when they're moist. Stick one to your top lip and one to your bottom lip and go …

"Quack!"

Now you're really starting to look and sound like a duck.

Flap your arms and try a sort of waddling walk. Practise this at home. When you're really confident that you could be mistaken for a duck, head down to the duck pond and see if the ducks will accept you as one of their own. Don't get eaten by a fox, though – I've heard that can happen if your duck impression is too convincing.

That looks more like a seagull, Harry.

Yeah, I know…

Check it out here:

DAY 333

Write some new silly nursery rhymes

Rewrite nursery rhymes to bring them up to date, so instead of Old Macdonald running a farm, what if he now runs a computer repair shop?

> Old Macdonald had a computer repair shop,
> E-I-E-I-O!
> And in his shop he had a laptop,
> E-I-E-I-O!
> With a tap-tap here and a tap-tap there,
> Here a tap,
> There a tap,
> Everywhere a tap-tap.
> Old Macdonald had a computer repair shop,
> E-I-E-I-O!

What if Mary didn't have a little lamb but some other pet?

> Mary had a little newt
> She rescued from a well,
> And everywhere that Mary went,
> The newt made quite a smell!*

* I think the newt was nervous being out of the well.

THAT'S MY NEWT!

MARY BERRY →

Hey! I'm not THAT small!

Try changing the lyrics to some of these nursery rhymes:

* "Twinkle Twinkle Little Star"
* "I'm a Little Teapot"
* "London Bridge Is Falling Down"
* "Humpty Dumpty Sat on a Wall"
* "Hey Diddle Diddle"
* "Baa Baa Black Sheep"

DAY 334

Make your nan look ten years younger

NAN BEFORE / AFTER
SELLOTAPE FACE LIFT

It's a privilege to get older, of course, but sometimes I'm sure older people occasionally look in the mirror and wish they looked a tad younger. Well, the good news is all they need is a visit from you and your roll of Sellotape!

Make sure they're up for it and sitting comfortably — and keep them away from any mirrors — that'll spoil the surprise.

Pull bits of your grandparent's face up — back to where they were when they were younger — and secure them in place with strips of Sellotape. Once you're happy with their new look, hand them a mirror and say, "Ta-dah!"

DAY 335

Ask your neighbour for a favour

Have you seen my noodlebury nuts?

No!

Next time you visit a neighbours' house, ask them for random, imaginary items. Say things like: "Sorry to bother you, but my mum's making a cake. Have you got any noodlebury nuts?" or "Excuse me, my dad's doing some DIY and wants to know whether you've got a Dingleswot tool he can borrow?"

Or even… "Our dog's got sunburn. Do you have any spare clouds?"

Make a note of their reactions and enjoy the puzzled looks you receive.

DAY 336

Get a selfie with the silliest thing you can find

Find the silliest thing you can and say, "Oh my gosh, it's you! You're so famous!" and then ask them for a selfie.

DAY 337

Paint a silly portrait

Today we're going to be painting or drawing someone's portrait – but because this is a silly year, it's going to be a silly portrait.

Ask a friend or auntie whether they'd like you to do their portrait. The more serious you appear at this stage, the funnier it will be when you reveal what you've been up to.

Tell them to take a seat and then take a long time setting up – if you've got an easel, great. If not, no problem – get your pencils or brushes and paints laid out on a small table or tray, a jar of water – as much stuff as you can find.

Spend some time getting them to pose in the right way with instructions like: "Can you put your arm up two inches, please?" and "Can you give me a slightly more mysterious smile?" Then set to work on your portrait, but make sure they can't see what you're up to.

When you're ready and enough time has elapsed to raise their expectations sky high, reveal your creation: a smiley face emoji! Then say, "Well, what do you think?"

DAY 338

Try brushtalking

Carry a toothbrush with you and whenever you're about to talk to someone, whip it out and, as you talk, brush your teeth at the same time.

DAY 339

Bristle fun

Get hold of some shaving foam – either buy some or borrow your mum's. When the doorbell goes, quickly lather your face up with foam and answer it, saying, "Sorry about this – I was just having a shave!"

DAY 340

Wear odd shoes

Wear a different shoe on each foot – pair up a flip-flop with a wellie, or a sandal with a trainer, or a leather school shoe with a Croc.

SHOE SERVING SUGGESTION

DAY 341

Airport message-go-round

It's so boring waiting for your luggage at the airport, isn't it? Well, here's a way to liven up your time at the luggage carousel. Put a series of handwritten notes on it every few minutes, and as they roll by, watch people's faces as they read them.

Messages like:

* Hi there! I'm the luggage carousel!
* Sorry to keep you waiting!
* I really like your hair!
* Not long now!
* I never get to go on holiday!

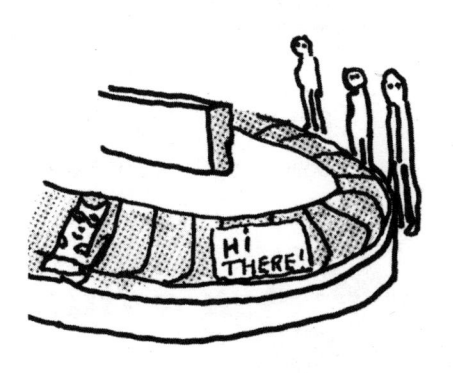

Or whatever you think the carousel would say if it could talk.

SILLY FACT NUMBER 18

Hiccups are actually baby ghosts trying to make themselves heard.

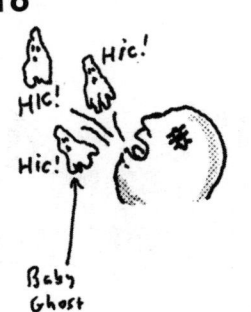

DAY 342

Eat a whole jar of mustard (not really)

Take an empty jar of mustard – wash it out and fill it with yoghurt mixed with some yellow food colouring. Pop it in the fridge to keep it nice and cool.

The next time someone comes round, offer them the mustard with a spoon: "Fancy some mustard?" They will, of course, turn their nose up and say "No thanks!" and "You must be joking!" Then you shrug and tuck in – slurping down as much phoney mustard as you can get in your mouth. "Mmmmm! Yum-yum!"

DAY 343

Ask a dummy

Ask a mannequin in a clothes shop for directions.

DAY 344

Oh Mother!

Go up to someone and say, "Mum?"

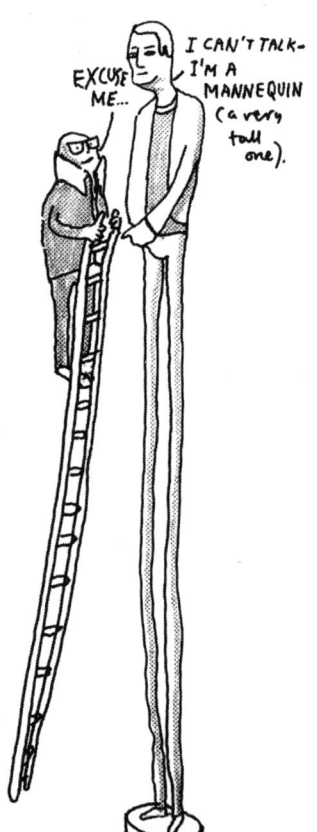

DAY 345

Strictly Come Toothbrush

Have a toothbrush dance-off with your family members. Put on some music, grab your toothbrushes and dance like nobody's watching, but with your toothbrushes as dance partners. Who can come up with the craziest toothbrush moves?

DAY 346

Hair today, gone tomorrow

Challenge your friends and family to create the wackiest and most outrageous hairstyles using items you find around the house, like rubber bands, straws and paperclips. Take pictures and stick them in your scrapbook.

DAY 347

Make a joke book

Read a book on the bus or train that you've made a fake cover for, so it's now called *How to Read*. Maybe start by trying to read it upside down.

DAY 348

Try this silly paper bag trick

I first saw this very silly trick on TV way back in the 1970s when a very famous comedy double act called Morecambe and Wise* did it.

Take a regular brown paper bag – like the ones you get loose fruit and veg in from the supermarket.

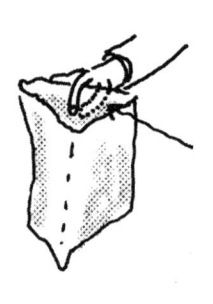

Holding the bag between your thumb and your middle finger, reach into the bag with your other hand and pretend to fetch something out of it. Then throw this imaginary object up into the air. Move the bag under where you think it would fall (if it was real!) and click the fingers holding the bag – to anyone watching, it looks like something just fell into the bag from a great height!

Reach into the bag again and repeat it a couple of times, then hand the bag to the person watching and see if they can do it. I bet they can't!!!

* They're great! Look 'em up on YouTube!

DAY 349

Remote-controlled dog

Take your dog (or a friend's dog) to the park and let him off the lead – obviously only if you know he'll come back! Pretend you're controlling the dog with one of those joysticks from a computer game or a remote-controlled car. This also works with a goldfish or duck but not with a cat.

DAY 350

Make a silly commemorative plate

Decorate a white plate with coloured whiteboard pens, celebrating all the silly things that you've done so far.

SILLY PEOPLE FROM HISTORY NUMBER 4: WILLIAM BUCKLAND

Buckland (1784–1856) filled his house with every kind of animal he could get his hands on and then ate them – including a crocodile and a mouse. He said that flies and moles tasted the worst.

WILLIAM BUCKLAND

DAY 351

Make a celebrity breadstick dispenser

← Breadstick

We all love celebrities, right? And we all love breadsticks, so why not combine the two to create a celebrity breadstick dispenser.

* Print off a picture of a celeb's face – or cut one out from a magazine cover, or draw your own version of them. Glue it onto a piece of card.

* Cut a hole around their mouth, just big enough to take a breadstick.

* Glue two fruit pastilles near the bottom of the piece of card, ideally a red one and a green one.

* Under the green ones write "ON" and under the red ones write "OFF".

* Go up to your family and friends* and ask them whether they'd like a breadstick (believe me, they will).

---

* If you've still got any left at this stage in the year!

* Tell them to press the "ON" button, at which point start feeding the breadstick slowly through the hole in the mouth. Tell them to press the "OFF" button when they've got enough breadstick for their needs. When they press "OFF", stop feeding the breadstick through and let them break off their breadstick – that's theirs to keep! And that's the Celebrity Breadstick Dispenser in a nutshell!

Of course, you could use any celebrity face and make any kind of dispenser – it doesn't have to be breadsticks! Here are some variations:

* The Amanda Holden Breadstick Dispenser
* The Alan Sugar Liquorice Bootlace Dispenser
* The Queen Camilla Sausage Dispenser
* The Bradley Walsh Brazil Nut Dispenser

HOW IT WORKS
(You push a breadstick through a hole.)

DAY 352

Help a duck go swimming

Get some feathers from an old cushion or pillow and stand by the duck pond with them in your hands. If anyone asks, just say you're holding a duck's clothes while it goes for a swim.

DAY 353

Take it in turns to write a story

This is a good one for car journeys. One person starts a story and then you go round the car taking it in turns to add the next sentence. The goal is to create the silliest story possible. It ends when someone says, "And they all lived happily ever after."

I'd love to know what you come up with.

HARRY:	Once upon a time there was a bald man with glasses.
STOUFFER:	Who got his foot caught in the washing machine!

DAY 354

Come up with a chocolate-based measuring system

I like centimetres and inches, but wouldn't it be more fun if we had a measuring system based on chocolate bars? Use a chocolate bar to measure stuff in your house.

One choc bar = Three Brazil nuts

* How tall's your dad? (Mine is 18 chocolate bars).
* How long is your sofa? (Mine is 22 chocolate bars).
* How long is your mum's nose? (My mum's nose is 2.5 chocolate bars — she's had a very long nose since she got it caught in the car door.)

You don't have to choose chocolate bars as your unit of measurement — you could choose spaghetti, Twiglets, guitars ... or absolutely anything!

SILLY FACT NUMBER 22

You use twice as much energy swimming as you do running. That's why it's OK to take a piece of cake into the swimming pool.

DAY 355

Make a multi-purpose stick

It's so tricky to think of original Christmas presents, isn't it? They're expensive too. Why spend money on friends and family when you could be spending it on silly stuff or sweets for yourself?

The good news is, I've found a great cheap alternative to expensive presents, which will really cheer up your family and friends – well, maybe not friends so much. Sticks! Yes, you read that correctly, sticks!

Go to the park or the wood – or anywhere there's a tree – and pick up sticks. Your ideal stick is 18–30 cm long and about as wide as a finger.*

When you get your sticks home, give them a bath to clean off any mud or bugs and dry them off with some paper towel. Get a piece of cardboard and trim it so it's 3 cm bigger than the stick all the way round. Tape the stick to the piece of card and write on the card "MULTI-PURPOSE STICK". Then write a list of all the things you can use the stick for.

← A STICK in a TOWELLING Bath ROBE after it has had a bath

---

* Not a fish finger, though – that's far too wide.

Here are a few suggestions – but I'm sure you'll come up with some of your own:

MULTI-PURPOSE STICK!

Ideal for:

- Poking things
- Stirring liquids – including paint
- Pointing at stuff
- Pressing buttons or doorbells
- Fuel for a fire

Maybe include some things you shouldn't do with the stick like …

DO NOT USE FOR:

- Wafting
- As a buoyancy aid
- As a key

Then cover your cardboard-mounted stick in cling film and you've got yourself a humorous novelty gift for Christmas.

To really increase appreciation of the stick, put a sticker on it with a very high price (maybe £25?), then make it look like you've tried to cross the price out! That way they'll think they're getting a really premium, top-of-the-range Christmas gift. Sorted!

DAY 356

Start a stop race

How come all running races start from a stationary position? How about starting on the move and the winner is the person who's got the furthest?

Try it out for me, would you? Stage a race with some friends – you all start running and someone else shouts,

"On your marks, get set, stop!"

Let me know if it works.

DAY 357

Tie your dad to a chair

The next time your dad or other relative falls asleep whilst watching a romantic comedy or *The Repair Shop*, quietly run round them with a ball of wool and tie them around their waist to their chair! Only agree to untie them in exchange for:

1. Sweets
2. Money
3. If they promise not to shout at you

DAY 358

Being silly at Christmas

Christmas is great, isn't it? What do you mean, "It goes on a bit, especially when I didn't get the presents I asked for. I wanted an Xbox but my parents bought me an egg box?" Well, here is a silly thing you can do to keep yourself entertained whilst the rest of your family tuck into cold meat.

Silly Christmas speech

Why should the King be the only one to make a speech at Christmas? Remember, you are the king or queen of Bedroomville!* Write and perform your own speech and film it so it looks as "official" as possible – you know, put a tie on or a fancy outfit, maybe even a crown if you can get one (there's usually one in a Christmas cracker), sit at a desk, put a photo of your mum and dad in a frame next to you, and off you go.

* See Day 96...

You can make your speech as funny as you like; talk about stuff that's happened to you and your family. Make sure at the end you wish everyone a very merry Christmas.

DAY 359

Turn a marrow into a squirty gun

Ask an adult to help you cut the end off a marrow and hollow out the centre bit where the seeds are, then fill it with shaving foam. Make a small hole (about half a centimetre) in the other end. Cut the end off a cucumber and place it into the marrow.

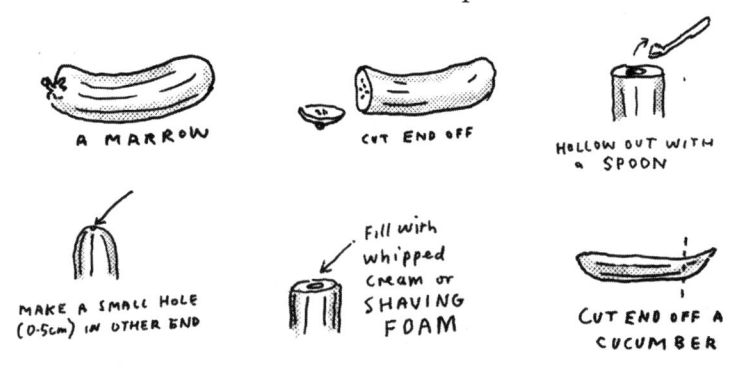

A MARROW

CUT END OFF

HOLLOW OUT WITH a SPOON

MAKE A SMALL HOLE (0·5cm) IN OTHER END

Fill with whipped cream or SHAVING FOAM

CUT END OFF A CUCUMBER

Take your marrow gun outside and point the marrow at whatever you're hoping to fire it at – I suggest a paper target stuck to a tree, but it could be your dad or your least favourite teddy bear.

Plunge the cucumber into the marrow as fast as you can, and the shaving foam will squirt out of the end in a jet! The harder and faster you push the cucumber, the further the foam will go.

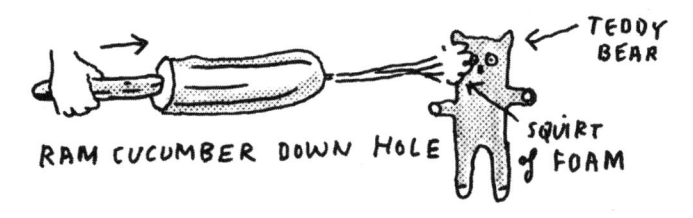

RAM CUCUMBER DOWN HOLE

TEDDY BEAR

SQUIRT of FOAM

DAY 360

Sleep with your eyes open

Paint eyes on your eyelids using washable face paints, or cut life-sized eyes out of photos in magazines, lick the back of them and stick them on your closed eyelids.

Draw eyes on the eyelids

WEIRD FACE!

When you close your eyes, people will think you're still awake. This is very useful in a maths lesson, or if you want to avoid talking to your auntie.

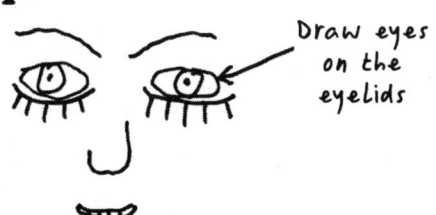

Note

Eyes are sensitive, so gently does it with this one.

DAY 361

Point at the metal horse

When a train goes by, point at it and shout, "Metal horse! Metal horse!"

DAY 362

Mash-up

We're nearly there! You've been silly for almost a whole year! To celebrate, make some silly potatoes, bake them in the oven, then eat them with a knob of butter – delicious! Even better with sausages. This will remind you of all the fun you've had in the past year.

I don't want to be cooked!

Why are you smiling then?

DAY 363

Make up your own silly thing to do

I've done enough work! With the training you've had over the course of the year, you should now be ready to come up with your own silly ideas. I'd love to hear them!

I hope you enjoyed this book — make sure you let me know your SILLY IDEAS!

DAY 364

Silly self-assessment

Go back to the silly assessment you did on **Day 1** and see if you're any sillier now than when you started this book. Let's hope so — otherwise the whole thing has been a complete waste of time!

*Silly self-assessment scores**

SCORE 0–5

Not very silly at all. You've got a lot of work to do – if you don't pull your socks up (and your pants for that matter), you're destined to go through life being very serious. I'll be honest, I'm seriously worried about you – and you know me, I don't like being serious. You need to start on these tasks straight away.

SCORE 5–10: Quite silly

Don't be disappointed by this score – it's the most common result in someone of your age group. You do some silly things occasionally, but a lot of the time you're quite serious – so there is a lot of room for improvement. The good news is you're really going to get a lot out of this book. Think of yourself as a serious caterpillar – by the end of this book, you're going to be a very silly butterfly. If you scored 0–5 in this test, why are you reading this bit? I told you to start right away!

SCORE 10–15

That's what I scored! I wonder what it means?

* The correct answer for each question is the last box in each list!

Tell me, Adrian, did you really hate this book?

I haven't had this much <u>FUN</u> for AGES, Harry! But don't tell anyone!

He! He! He! He!

Adrian's first smile!

DAY 365

Congratulations, you made it!

You have been silly for a whole year! Your last silly challenge is: make yourself a very silly certificate.

Every now and then, flick through your scrapbook of madness and think to yourself...

Did this really happen?

DAY 366

Leap year bonus activity

Spot the five differences in this super-silly-mega-extra bonus activity.

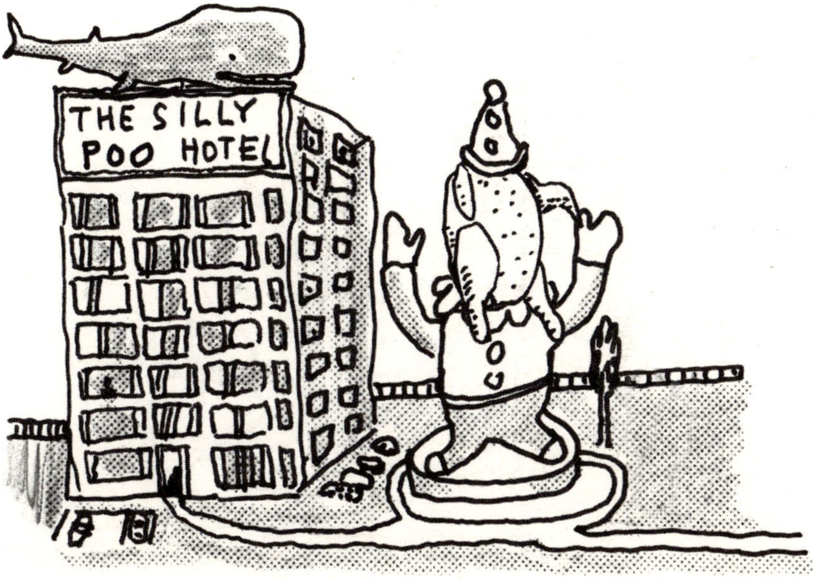
THE SILLY
POO HOTEL

Biography

Harry Hill is a multiple award-winning comedian, presenter and author. He is one of the UK's most respected and inventive entertainers. Starting with his own ingenious comedy series on BBC2 and Channel 4, he went on to create the hit ITV series *Harry Hill's TV Burp*, which ran for ten years. He has been the longstanding voice of ITV's *You've Been Framed* and is the presenter of Channel 4's *Junior Bake Off*. As an author, Harry has written several bestselling joke books, and amongst others, the popular children's series Matt Millz. He is also an artist and has shown his work at the Royal Academy. Harry's brand-new podcast, "Are We There Yet?" is the world's first family-friendly podcast packed with jokes, fun facts and so much more.

Find out more at: harryhill.co.uk

"How do you think it went STOUFF'?"

"OK!"

THIS IS the BACK